T0303933

Energy Policy in China

Energy policy has always been an important part of China's national policy agenda. Although the overall Chinese economy has become largely market-driven, its energy sectors are still subject to varying degrees of government control. Authoritarian governance allows China to move very quickly in some areas, such as hydropower, nuclear power, wind power, and solar energy. However, conflicting interests have also led to infighting and impasses.

With a specific focus on energy supply, *Energy Policy in China* provides a succinct account of China's energy policy over the last sixty years. Using separate chapters dedicated to each energy sub-sector, Chi-Jen Yang introduces and discusses both the achievements and failures of the Chinese energy systems, as well as the strengths and insufficiencies of energy governance in China.

This book is an interdisciplinary study written for a broad audience, including those researching and working in the fields of energy policy, business strategy, and government administration, as well as Chinese and Asian Studies more broadly.

Chi-Jen Yang is an Independent Energy Consultant and was previously a Research Scientist at the Center on Global Change, Duke University, USA. He holds a Ph.D. in Public Affairs from Princeton University, USA and three master degrees from the Massachusetts Institute of Technology, USA and National Taiwan University, Taiwan.

Routledge Studies in Energy Policy

Energy Policy in China

Chi-Jen Yang

LONDON AND NEW YORK

First published 2017
by Routledge
2 Park Square, Milton Park, Abingdon, Oxon OX14 4RN

and by Routledge
711 Third Avenue, New York, NY 10017

Routledge is an imprint of the Taylor & Francis Group, an informa business

British Library Cataloguing-in-Publication Data
A catalogue record for this book is available from the British Library

Library of Congress Cataloging-in-Publication Data
A catalog record for this book has been requested

ISBN: 978-1-138-08052-2 (hbk)
ISBN: 978-1-315-11341-8 (ebk)

Typeset in Times New Roman
by Apex CoVantage, LLC

Contents

Figures

Tables

1 Introduction

The sheer size of China's energy economy makes it an extremely important topic. Since 2009, China has surpassed the United States as the world's largest energy consumer (Figure 1.1). No matter if you like it or hate it, China has become the most important country in the global energy arena.

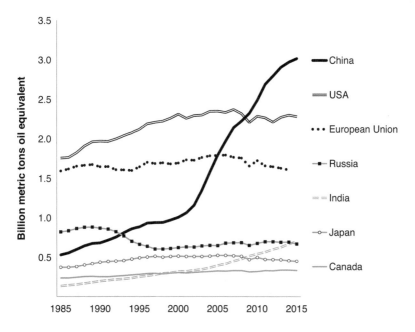

Figure 1.1 Total primary energy consumption of the largest consuming countries and European Union

Source: BP (2016); World Bank (2017)

Energy, economy, and carbon emissions

Although China has already become the largest energy economy in the world, it still has tremendous potential of further growth. The historical trajectories of developed economies (Figure 1.2) consistently show that in the early stages of economic development, the increases of per capita Gross Domestic Product (GDP) were always accompanied by the increases of per capita energy consumption. The decoupling between economic growth and increasing energy consumption occurs only after the economy has reached a certain level of maturity. Each country's level of maturity differs due to the differences in natural resource endowments, infrastructure, lifestyles, and government policies, but the overall patterns are rather similar.

On a per capita basis, China is still by far poorer than the developed economies. It is still in a relatively early stage of economic development. Although China's growth in energy consumption has significantly slowed down since 2014 (Qi et al., 2016), it is not yet clear whether it will stabilize at such a low level.

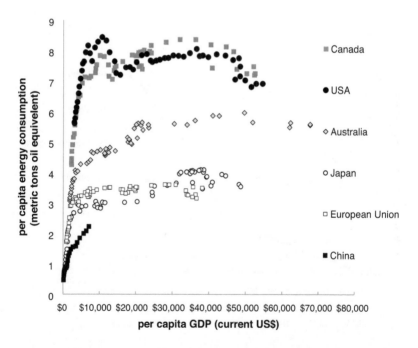

Figure 1.2 Per capita energy consumption versus per capita GDP in major countries and regions (1960–2014)

Source: World Bank (2017)

Because energy use is the most dominant source of carbon dioxide (CO_2) emissions, the trajectories of CO_2 emissions are highly correlated with those of energy consumption (Figure 1.3). As the Chinese economy continues to develop, its CO_2 emissions will most likely keep rising. China's contribution in global CO_2 emissions has gradually increased from about 4% in the 1960s to about 14% in 2000, and has reached 29% in 2013. China is now by far the largest greenhouse gas–emitting country in the world (Figure 1.4).

Because global warming is the common challenge of humankind, the energy policy of China should be humankind's common concern. To a very significant extent, Chinese policymakers are deciding the direction of our common future as a global society. Not only do people of other countries have no influence on energy policy in China; most of them are hardly aware of what is happening. Available information about energy policy in China outside the Chinese-speaking communities is grossly inadequate. I hope this book will help bridge the gap.

The purpose of this book is to provide a concise and yet relatively comprehensive introduction to China's energy policy in a storytelling manner, with narratives that are accurate, straightforward, and interesting. This book is primarily a description of the history and evolution of Chinese energy

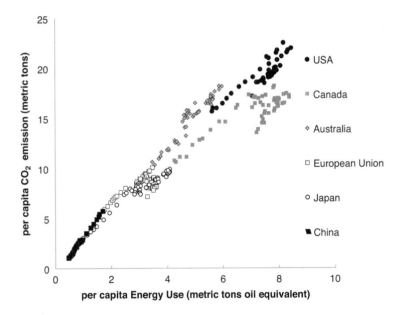

Figure 1.3 Per capita CO_2 emissions versus per capita energy use in major countries and regions (1960–2014)

Source: World Bank (2017)

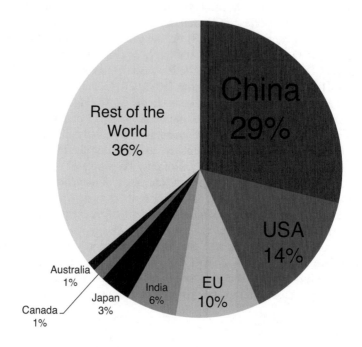

Figure 1.4 Breakdowns of global CO_2 emissions in 2013
Source: World Bank (2017)

policy, rather than a critique of it. I try to minimize the injection of personal opinions, or so-called "insights." Readers should find that this book contains much more information but less insights than others on similar topics. The contents in this book are empirical and not organized according to any theoretical framework. They are simply true stories in the history of China's energy policy. The history is not selectively represented or structured to prove or disapprove any particular theories. They are simply meant to introduce this very important subject to whoever is interested.

Current energy mix

The energy system in China is very different from those in the developed countries (Figure 1.5). China is far more dependent on coal than the rest of the world. Despite its very rapid development of renewable energy in recent years, non-hydro renewable energy contributed only 2% of China's primary energy consumption in 2015. China still has a very long way to

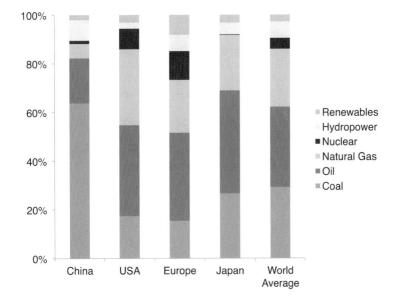

Figure 1.5 Breakdowns of primary energy consumption by fuel in 2015
Source: BP (2016)

go in its transition to low-carbon economy. Despite being applauded as the leader in developing renewable energy, the share of non-hydro renewables in China's 2015 energy mix indeed lagged behind Europe, the United States, Japan, and the world average.

Energy governance

The political system in China is dramatically different from those in the developed countries. As a result, its energy governance also differs greatly. The rule of law is not commonly respected in China. Despite its authoritarian nature, the Chinese government's laws and policies are not always followed. Many scholars have described the Chinese governance as fragmented authoritarianism (Lieberthal, 1995; Brødsgaard, 2017), which points out both its authoritarian nature and inconsistence among different parts of the authority. Phillips Andrews-Speed argues that China's transition to a low-carbon economy is highly constrained by its prevailing institutions (Andrews-Speed, 2012). In this book, I do not argue for or against those views. I simply tell the stories, describe what happened, and leave the judgment to the readers.

References

Andrews-Speed, C.P., 2012. *The Governance of Energy in China: Transition to a Low-Carbon Economy*. Palgrave Macmillan, Basingstoke

BP, 2016. *Statistical Review of World Energy*. BP, London

Brødsgaard, K.E., 2017. *Chinese Politics as Fragmented Authoritarianism: Earthquakes, Energy and Environment*. Routledge, New York

Lieberthal, K., 1995. *Governing China: From Revolution Through Reform*. Norton, New York; London

Qi, Y., Stern, N., Wu, T., Lu, J., Green, F., 2016. China's post-coal growth. *Nature Geoscience* 9, 564–566

World Bank, *World Development Indicators*. http://databank.worldbank.org/data/reports.aspx?source=world-development-indicators (accessed 2/8/2017)

2 Historical context

Since the People's Republic of China (PRC) was founded in 1949, it has restructured and reformed its economic institutions several times and in many aspects. The purpose of this chapter is to familiarize readers with the underlying political and economic context. In order to better understand the evolution of energy policies, they must be put in the context of broader political economy.

The economic reform that started in 1978 marked the most important divide in the history of the PRC. From 1949 to 1978, the Chinese economy was largely a Soviet-style planned economy. After 1978, the Chinese government started to introduce market mechanisms in more and more sectors and gradually revised its laws, regulations, and rules to be more consistent with those in the developed countries.

Soviet-style planned-economy (1949–1978)

After the Chinese Communist Party succeeded in the revolution and established the People's Republic of China in 1949, their goal was to build a Soviet-style planned economy. However, after over a decade of wars, first with Japanese invaders and then the civil war with the Nationalist Party (Kuomintang) regime, the Chinese economy was severely wrecked. In the first few years of the PRC, rehabilitation of infrastructure and restoration of production were more urgent than the reform toward public ownership and planned economy. From 1949 to 1952, the PRC government allowed public and private ownership to coexist and welcomed capitalists to stay.

Back then, China had a very small energy industry. In 1949, the Ministry of Fuel Industry was established to be in charge of planning and production of fuels, and the Ministry of Water Resources was in charge of hydropower. With aide from the Soviet Union, the economic restoration proceeded quickly and successfully. From 1949 to 1952, China's power generation

Table 2.1 Restoration of energy production 1949–1952

	1949	1952
Installed electric capacity (GW)	1.85	1.97
Power generation (TWh)	4.3	7.3
Coal production (million metric tons)	32	66
Crude oil production (thousand metric tons)	120	436

Source: Wang (2009); Hu (2016)

Table 2.2 Key energy indicators in the First Five-Year Plan

	1952	1957
Installed electric capacity (GW)	1.97	4.64
Power generation (TWh)	7.3	19.3
Coal production (million metric tons)	66	131
Crude oil production (thousand metric tons)	436	1449

Source: Wang (2009); Hu (2016)

was increased by 69%, coal production more than doubled, and crude oil more than tripled (Table 2.1).

Communist China's transition toward public ownership and planned economy started during the First Five-Year Plan (1953–1957). Farmers were encouraged or pressured to join agricultural cooperatives, and private factories and shops were also turned into cooperatives. Private property ownership was essentially eliminated. By the end of the First Five-Year Plan, the Chinese economy was transformed into a Soviet-style planned economy.

The centerpiece of the First Five-Year Plan was the construction of 156 large industrial projects, with technologies and equipment imported from the Soviet Union and Eastern Europe. A significant share of the 156 projects was energy-related, including 24 power plants, 25 coal mining and processing projects, and 2 oil refineries.

The Soviet Union economy grew rapidly in the 1950s (Ofer, 1987), so did its copied version in China. From 1952 to 1957, China's power generation and coal output more than doubled, and crude oil production more than tripled (Table 2.2).

Encouraged by the spectacular success of planned economy, the Chinese Communist leaders decided to set very aggressive targets in the Second Five-Year Plan (1958–1962). From 1958 to 1961, the Communist Party

Table 2.3 Energy performances in the Second Five-Year Plan and the Great Leap
Forward targets

	1957	1962 actual result	1962 target
Installed electric capacity (GW)	4.6	13	74
Power generation (TWh)	19.3	45.8	100
Coal production (million metric tons)	131	220	900
Crude oil production (thousand metric tons)	1449	5749	50,000

Source: Wang (2009); Hu (2016)

mobilized the social and economic campaign called "Great Leap Forward," which aimed at very rapid industrialization and the transformation of China into a socialist society. The Great Leap Forward aimed to increase most of agricultural and industrial outputs by 10 times or more (Table 2.3). The energy targets were particularly ambitious (Yang, 2008).

The core of the Great Leap Forward was steel production. In order to very quickly ramp up the production of steel, Chinese policymakers pursued a "walking on two legs" approach, which was to utilize both simple traditional technology as well as advanced industrial one. In addition to large industrial steel furnaces, numerous small backyard furnaces were built in every commune and neighborhood. In order to supply fuels to the widespread backyard furnaces, villagers developed numerous small coal mines. The ubiquitous and disperse development of small coal mines eventually lead to the fragmented organizational structure of China's coal mining sector.

The overemphasis on increasing industrial outputs at the expenses of the livelihoods of the people made the Second Five-Year statistics seemingly impressive on paper, while the actual human conditions were catastrophic. In the overzealous pursuit of unrealistically high industrial outputs, tremendous resources and manpower were diverted from agricultural production. The result was a severe shortage of food. Numerous useful metal tools were melted into scrap metal in backyard furnaces for the sake of boosting steel outputs. The government directly controlled all economic activities and behaved foolishly, and millions of people starved to death.

The Great Leap Forward also triggered the Sino-Soviet split, which was the sudden deterioration of China-Soviet Union relation. In 1960, the Soviet Union withdrew all its advisors from China, due to its concerns of China's dangerous Great Leap Forward. Mao Zedong, however, interpreted the withdrawal of personnel as a betrayal and accused the Soviet advisors for causing the famine.

The political struggle among the Chinese Communist leaders, unfortunately, prolonged Mao's dictatorship. In 1959, Liu Shaoqi replaced Mao Zedong as the State Chairman, while Mao retained his position as the Communist Party chairman. In 1961, Liu Shaoqi ended the Great Leap Forward movement and criticized the mistakes in Mao's policy, and revised policies. In 1965, Liu was re-elected as the State Chairman.

In 1966, Mao Zedong launched the Cultural Revolution, which started with a coup d'état to resume leadership and purge Liu Shaoqi from both the government and the party. Liu was arrested and tortured to death. Mao denied his mistakes in the Great Leap Forward and blamed the famine on natural disasters.

The turmoil of the Great Leap Forward caused a three-year hiatus in regular national planning. The Third Five-Year Plan (1966–1970) did not start until 1966. The Third and Fourth (1971–1975) Five-Year Plans were during the Cultural Revolution, when autarky and austerity were the guiding economic principles. Each region developed their own energy resources to be self-sufficient.

The Cultural Revolution promoted Mao to godlike status. Many top government leaders, most notably Liu Shaoqi and Deng Xiaoping, were expelled. Millions of people were persecuted violently. It was a political and ideological mobilization of unprecedented scale and duration. However, the economic impact was surprisingly limited. At the end of the Cultural Revolution, rural villagers remained poor but no longer starved. Primary education has expanded significantly and literacy rate increased greatly. Basic health care became widely available. Industrial production also expanded greatly, although the technologies were backward and inefficient.

In terms of energy production, the growth was quite spectacular (Table 2.4). Although China's standards of living lagged much behind its East Asian neighbors, its planned era had paved a good foundation for economic take-off once the market forces were unleashed.

Table 2.4 Key energy indicators in the Third and Fourth Five-Year Plans

	1965	1970	1975
Installed electric capacity (GW)	15.1	23.8	43.4
Power generation (TWh)	67.6	115.9	195.8
Coal production (million metric tons)	231	354	482
Crude oil production (thousand metric tons)	11331	30586	77127

Source: NBS (2010); Hu (2016)

Reform and opening up (since 1978)

Mao Zedong died in September 1976. After a short transitional period headed by Hua Guofeng, Deng Xiaoping assumed the leadership of China. Deng initiated the "Reform and Opening Up" policy, which was to introduce market mechanisms into the Chinese economy and open up to international trade and foreign investments.

Unlike the "shock therapy" or "big bang" economy reforms pursued by many Eastern European countries and Russia, Deng adopted a gradual and cautious approach in China's transition from a dominantly planned economy to a relatively market-driven one (Naughton, 2007). The energy sector is considered to be of strategic importance to national security, and therefore was among the last to be reformed.

Deng's economic reform started with agriculture. While rural lands remains collectively owned, the rights to use the lands were divided and contracted to individual households. Farmers were allowed to keep their outputs after paying a certain share to the state. The above-plan outputs were sold in free market, where prices were typically higher than the planned price. The coexistence of planned and market economies, also known as the dual-track system, was gradually adopted in more and more economic sectors. Over time, the share of market-priced output tends to grow much faster than the planned output. Once the planned share of a particular sector becomes insignificant, the planning practice may be abolished.

China's economic reform quickly expanded from agriculture to village and township enterprises in 1979. In 1981, small private businesses with less than eight employees became allowed. The market economy continued to expand.

In 1988, the National People's Congress passed a constitutional amendment to officially legalize private enterprises. Over time, the private sector has grown to be the dominant contributor in the overall Chinese economy. In 2011, the state-owned and state-controlled industries' share of industrial output has dropped to 26% (Lardy, 2014). However, the energy sector is an exception. In 2011, state-owned and state-controlled industries accounted for 54% of coal output, 92% of oil and gas, and 93% of electric power. Nevertheless, being state-owned or state-controlled does not necessarily mean that they are not market-driven.

During the 1980s and 1990s, the Chinese government gradually separated the business functions from government administrations and reorganized the business assets as state-owned corporations. The state-owned assets in the same business were typically divided into several companies to create a competitive environment. However, the state energy companies are run by politically appointed managers, and the government still issues directives and guidance to the state-owned businesses from time to time. The operations of these state-owned corporations are neither completely market-driven nor entirely government-planned. The following chapters will introduce the situation in each energy sector.

The government administration of energy industries has been reorganized many times. Table 2.5 summarizes the major energy-related ministries in each period.

Table 2.5 Reorganization of major energy-related ministries

Year	Established	Abolished
1949	Ministry of Fuel Industry Ministry of Water Resources	
1955	Ministry of Coal Industry Ministry of Electric Power Industry Ministry of Petroleum Industry	Ministry of Fuel Industry
1958	Ministry of Water Resources and Electric Power	Ministry of Electric Power Industry Ministry of Water Resources
1970	Ministry of Fuel and Chemical Industry	Ministry of Coal Industry
1975	Ministry of Coal Industry Ministry of Petrochemical Industry	Ministry of Fuel and Chemical Industry
1978	Ministry of Petroleum Industry Ministry of Chemical Industry	Ministry of Petrochemical Industry
1979	Ministry of Water Resources Ministry of Electric Power Industry	Ministry of Water Resources and Electric Power
1980	National Energy Commission	
1982	Ministry of Water Resources and Electric Power China National Offshore Oil Corporation (CNOOC)	National Energy Commission Ministry of Water Resources Ministry of Electric Power Industry
1983	China Petroleum and Chemical Corporation (Sinopec)	
1988	Ministry of Energy Ministry of Water Resources China National Petroleum Corporation (CNPC/PetroChina)	Ministry of Water Resources and Electric Power Ministry of Coal Industry Ministry of Petroleum Industry Ministry of Nuclear Industry
1993	Ministry of Coal Industry Ministry of Electric Power Industry	Ministry of Energy

Year	Established	Abolished
1997	State Power Corporation	
1998		Ministry of Coal Industry Ministry of Electric Power Industry Ministry of Chemical Industry
2002	State Electricity Regulatory Commission Two State Grids: State Grid Corporation of China China Southern Power Grid Five Power Generation Groups: China Huaneng Group China Huadian Group Corporation China Guodian Corporation China Datang Corporation China Power Investment Corporation	State Power Corporation
2013	National Energy Administration	State Electricity Regulatory Commission

Five-Year Plans

The National Economic and Social Development Five-Year Plans, which are mentioned in many places in the book, are the overarching blueprints of China's national policy agenda. The early Five-Year Plans were highly centralized and single-minded on industrialization. After the economic reforms since 1978, the Five-Year Plans have become increasingly decentralized and multi-purposed. Environmental targets were first introduced in the Sixth Five-Year Plan, and since then have become increasingly important. Since the 11th Five-Year Plan, the national government started to prioritize the environment over the economy by making environmental targets legally binding while the economic targets are non-binding.

The target-responsibility system is an important mechanism in enforcing the targets in the Five-Year Plans. The State Council delegates the responsibilities of meeting the targets to the relevant departments and local governments. The quantitative national targets are broken up into a set of local and departmental targets. The local governments and functional departments participate in the target-setting process and negotiate for their shares of responsibilities. Once the targets are set, each local or departmental authority is responsible for meeting its designated target, and is punished if it misses the target.

Legally speaking, a Five-Year Plan is a periodically enacted law with preset five-year sunset clause. The drafting, implementation, and reviewing process of a Five-Year Plan provide an institutional framework for identifying and assessing urgent problems and formulating remedies. Like most developing countries, many of China's regular governance capacities are still grossly insufficient. The Five-Year Plans complement regular laws and regulations by addressing selected problems with more intense and focused political mobilizations.

Before 1998, the State Planning Commission was in charge of making the Five-Year Plans. The commission was renamed as National Development and Reform Commission (NDRC) in 1998. The NDRC always plays a pivotal role in China's national economic regulations and policies. It is technically equivalent to a ministry, but more influential than most ministries.

A Five-Year Plan cycle includes a series of consultations, internal policy discussions/debates, consensus forming, implementation, and performance reviews (Figure 2.1). The repeated cycles provide important opportunities for Chinese policymakers and government officials to exchange ideas and information, and to learn from past mistakes and improve their policies. Over time, the effectiveness of the Five-Year Plan has improved.

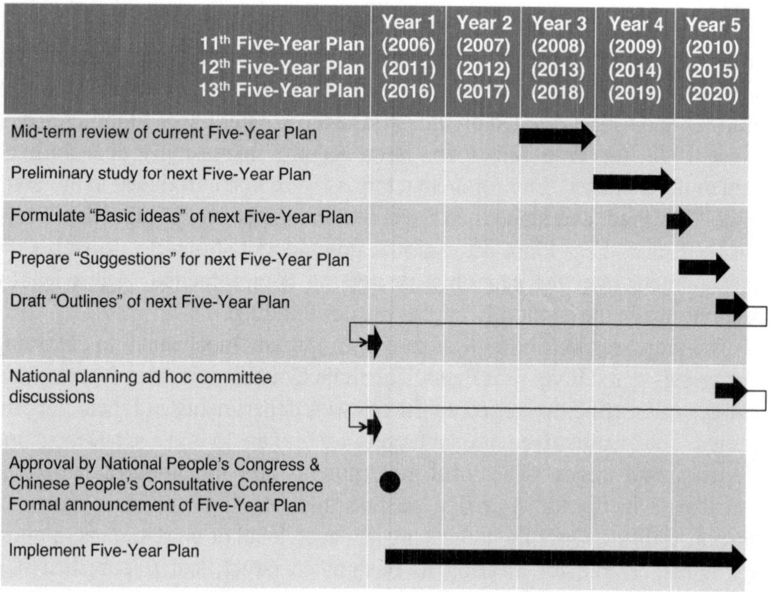

	Year 1 (2006) (2011) (2016)	Year 2 (2007) (2012) (2017)	Year 3 (2008) (2013) (2018)	Year 4 (2009) (2014) (2019)	Year 5 (2010) (2015) (2020)
11th Five-Year Plan / 12th Five-Year Plan / 13th Five-Year Plan					
Mid-term review of current Five-Year Plan			➡		
Preliminary study for next Five-Year Plan				➡	
Formulate "Basic ideas" of next Five-Year Plan					➡
Prepare "Suggestions" for next Five-Year Plan					➡
Draft "Outlines" of next Five-Year Plan	↳➡				➡
National planning ad hoc committee discussions	↳➡				➡
Approval by National People's Congress & Chinese People's Consultative Conference Formal announcement of Five-Year Plan	●				
Implement Five-Year Plan	➡➡➡➡➡➡➡➡➡➡➡➡➡				

Figure 2.1 Five-Year Plan cycle

Chapter highlights

- Energy has always been an important part of China's national policy agenda since the beginning of its planned economy.
- During the economic reform starting in 1978, the energy sector was among the last in the reform agenda.
- The Chinese government still exercises extensive control or influence over its energy industries.
- The Five-Year Plan has remained a very important instrument in China's energy and environmental policy.

References

CEC, 2016. *2015 National Power Industry Statistical Table*. China Electricity Council, Beijing (in Chinese: 2015 全国电力工业统计数据一览表, 中国电力企业联合会)

Hu, G., 2016. *Energy Institution Revolution: Introduction to Energy Policy Development in China*. Tsinghua University Press, Beijing (in Chinese: 能源体制革命: 中国能源政策发展概论)

Lardy, N.R., 2014. *Markets Over Mao: The Rise of Private Business in China*. Peterson Institute for International Economics, Washington, DC

Naughton, B., 2007. *The Chinese Economy: Transitions and Growth*. MIT Press, Cambridge, MA

NBS, 2010. *China Compendium of Statistics 1940–2008*. National Bureau of Statistics/China Statistics Press, Beijing (in Chinese: 新中国60年统计资料汇编)

Ofer, G., 1987. Soviet economic growth: 1928–1985. *Journal of Economic Literature* 25, 1767–1833

Wang, S., 2009. *One Hundred Years of Development in China's Petroleum Engineering*. www.cnpc.com.cn/syzs/sysh/201206/48a39f6d22d7430eba57f11b350603c8.shtml (in Chinese) (accessed 12/05/2016)

Yang, Q., 2008. History of thermal power construction and development in China (2). *Electric Power Construction* 29(2), 96–100 (in Chinese: 杨勤明, 2008. 中国火电建设发展史(2))

3 Coal

Coal is the largest source of energy in China. In 2015, coal accounted for 64% of China's total primary energy consumption. China is the world's largest coal producer and consumer. In 2015, China accounted for 48% of coal production and 50% of coal consumption in the world (BP, 2016). From 1949 to 2015, China's annual coal production increased 117 times, from 32 million to 3.75 billion metric tons. The trajectory of growth largely followed an exponential curve with two major deviations: the Great Leap Forward (1958–1961) and the 1997 Asian Financial Crisis (Figure 3.1).

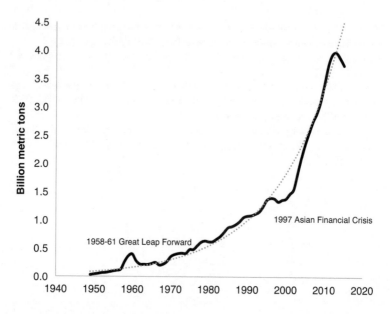

Figure 3.1 Coal production in China (1949–2015)

Source: NBS (2010); NBS (2016)

Small coal deposits are scattered throughout China. High-quality and large-scale coal resources, however, are highly concentrated in the north and northwest. China's energy demand centers are mostly in the coastal provinces in the east and southeast. The geographic mismatch between supply and demand of coal has always been a challenge to China's policymakers.

Because coal is the most important energy resource in China, it has always been a key component in China's economic policy. The center of the First Five-Year Plan (1952–1957) was the Soviet-assisted 156 large industrial projects, which included 25 large mechanized coal mining and processing facilities. During the Great Leap Forward (1958–1961), the "walking on two legs" policy was established to squeeze out more outputs. Under the "walking on two legs" principle, the government encourages both large industrial coal mines and small dispersed labor-intensive coal digging at almost every part of the country. The temporary boost of production with intensified political mobilization was proven unsustainable (Figure 3.1).

After a short recovery period following the Great Leap Forward, the Cultural Revolution (1966–1976) ensued. During this period, the Chinese government continued to pursue industrialization and development under the guiding principles of self-reliance and austerity. Due to the local self-sufficiency policy, numerous small coal mines were developed in regions with poor coal resources. These small dispersed coal mines are unsuitable for mechanized production. Not only do they have low outputs and require high labor inputs; they are also prone to mining accidents, and often cause damages to arable or grazing lands.

Before the 1978 economic reform, the state monopolized the procurement and distribution of coal. According to the Marxist doctrine, coal was not a commodity but a means of production. Because there was no market, price was a tool for accounting purpose only. In order to support industrial projects, the government intentionally set the coal price low. The coal mines operated with chronic financial losses or very low profits. From 1949 to 1978, the Chinese government only adjusted coal price twice (in 1958 and 1965). Coal producers had no incentive to deliver more than their assigned quotas. Despite the government's efforts to increase coal output through economic planning, shortages of coal were prevalent.

The economic reform for coal proceeded more cautiously than most other economic sectors. The dual-track scheme reform was not applied to coal until 1983. During the first year of reform, although coal producers were permitted to sell their surplus, free-market price was still not allowed. The above-plan coal price was higher but still administratively set. The within-quota coal price remained very low. In 1984, the price of above-plan coal output was decontrolled. The dual-track system continued for more than two decades. In the 1980s, China also began to allow local governments and private entities to invest in coal mining. In 1983 and 1984, the State Council announced policies to encourage the investment in small coal mines (Cao, 2008). Thousands of local private and public (provincial, township, and village) coal mines were built. By the 1990s, about 75,000–80,000 small coal mines were supplying roughly 45% of China's coal output (Andrews-Speed et al., 2003). As a result, the coal industry has become highly fragmented and the coal market increasingly competitive.

Coal mining safety

In the late 1980s and early 1990s, the government started to pay increasing attention to the problems of small coal mines, especially regarding the high death tolls of mining accidents. From 1989 to 1998, the coal mining policy focused on safety regulations. Despite the national government's repeated orders and notices to rectify safety violations, mining accidents remain frequent. Chinese township and village authorities typically have financial stakes in those local coal mines, and therefore are willing to relax or ignore safety regulations for economic gains. The central government's mining safety campaigns had little effect on local enforcement.

After the 1997 Asian Financial Crisis, the demand for coal declined significantly. The Chinese government seized the opportunity to eliminate the problematic small coal mines. In 1998, the State Council issued a notice to close down illegal and unreasonably located coal mines. By the end of 1999, the government reported the shutdown of 33,000 mines with the combined capacity of 300 million metric tons per year (Li, 2007). The campaign to close down small coal mines continued year after year. The government reportedly has closed 16,000 small coal mines in 2000 and 10,944 in 2001 (NBS, 2002). However, there were frequent reports of the supposedly closed mines resuming operation illegally. The number of mines that were actually closed remains unclear.

In June 2001, the State Council ordered all township and village coal mines to suspend production for safety rectification. In November 2001, a series of five coal mine explosions within 9 days killed 99 people in Shanxi province. All the explosions occurred at township and village coal mines where the production was supposedly suspended. Such incident indicated the ineffectiveness of national coal policy in China.

The arrival of Internet media, however, has a significant impact on local governance. Before the age of Internet, local authorities could easily censor local news media and cover up mining accidents. The availability of Internet makes such local censorship much more difficult, and the high death tolls of mining became a salient policy failure in China. In July 2001, a local attempt to cover up a mining accident of 81 deaths in Nandan, Guangxi, quickly escalated to a notorious scandal after the story was leaked out on the Internet (Peng, 2005).

The embarrassment of repeated policy failure of mining safety provided the national policymakers with much legitimacy to continue the closure of small coal mines. In 2005, the State Council announced its plan to completely restructure the coal mining industry within 3 to 5 years and shut down small coal mines that are unreasonably located, unfit for safe production, wasting resources, and damaging the environment.

According to the Chinese government's report, the number of small coal mines has gradually reduced from over 80,000 in the 1990s to 23,000 in 2005, and 7,000 in 2015 (Li, 2007; Economic Daily, 2016). China first spent about 40 years (1950s–1990s) on building more than 80,000 small coal mines, and then the following 20 years (1998–2017) on trying to get rid of them.

Coal price decontrol

The coal price decontrol was a very gradual process from roughly 1993 to 2005. In 1993, the planned coal price was abolished for all uses other than power generation. The government continued to convene annual contract meetings for major coal and power companies, setting a guiding price for electricity-purposed coal each year until 2001. From 2001 to 2004, the government renamed its guiding price as reference price, which implied a greater leeway for negotiation. In 2005, the Chinese government announced that it will no longer control the price of coal for power generation, which technically marked the end of coal price control in China.

After the price decontrol, coal prices continued to increase for about a decade (Figure 3.2), which is often dubbed as "Golden Decade of Coal" in Chinese media. During the "Golden Decade of Coal" (ca. 2002–2011), there were many news stories about the extravagant lifestyle of coal tycoons (VOC, 2016). The "new money" from coal quickly became a most envied and despised social class. The windfall profits of coal also lead to coal-rich local governments' generous fiscal policies. In 2009, Shenmu, Shaanxi, a coal mining city, became the first city in China to offer free health care to all. Ordos, Inner Mongolia, also a coal mining center, built China's largest ghost city, which soon became an global spectacle (Barboza, 2010; BBC, 2012). Inner Mongolia, the top coal producing region, ascended from one of the poorest regions to one of the richest in China during the Golden Decade.

Figure 3.2 China coal price versus Dubai oil price

Source: Yang et al. (2012); IMF (2016); Exbulk (2017)

Since the coal price decontrol, the price of coal has been rather volatile and largely moved in tandem with oil price (Yang et al., 2012). The price of coal has become largely market-driven, and the Chinese government no longer has the ability to dictate coal price. Nevertheless, the Chinese government has been unwilling to give up its attempts to intervene into the coal market. For example, in 2011, when the coal price rose above 800 RMB per metric ton, the National Development and Reform Commission (NDRC) announced a temporary price cap for electricity-purposed coal. In 2014, when coal prices were falling, the NDRC convened 18 meetings to "rescue" the coal industry (Wang, 2014).

In early 2016, the Chinese central government issued a series of executive orders, which were essentially the opposite of antitrust policy, to mandate and enforce a uniform 16% output reduction of all coal mines for the sake of increasing coal prices (NDRC, 2016; State Council, 2016). After the "anti-antitrust" (or "pro-trust") mandate was implemented, coal prices rose quickly in 2016. In November 2016, when the NDRC deemed that coal prices have risen too much, it convened a meeting to "alert and warn the coal industry regarding pricing behavior" (Shanghai Securities News, 2016).

In addition to the closure of small coal mines, the Chinese government has also encouraged mergers and acquisitions to consolidate the coal industry. The consolidation policy is another "anti-antitrust" policy, which aims to make the industry more concentrated (i.e., less competitive). Despite significant progress in the pro-trust policies, the coal sector has remained rather fragmented. Table 3.1 shows China's top 30 coal producers in 2015 and

Table 3.1 Top 30 coal producers and their market shares in 2015

Company name	2015 output (metric tons)	Market share (%)
Shenhua Group	433,260,000	11.7%
Datong Coal Mine Group	173,510,000	4.7%
China Coal	166,680,000	4.5%
Shandong Energy Group	133,680,000	3.6%
Shaanxi Coal and Chemical Industry	127,110,000	3.4%
Shanxi Coking Coal Group	105,350,000	2.9%
Yankuang Group	109,020,000	3.0%
Jizhong Energy Group	101,750,000	2.8%
Henan Coal Chemical Industry Group	107,630,000	2.9%
Kailuan Group	91,700,000	2.5%
Lu'An Group	86,380,000	2.3%
Yangquan Coal Industry	76,230,000	2.1%
Shanxi Jincheng Anthracite Mining Group	70,420,000	1.9%
Jinneng Group	70,360,000	1.9%
Huainan Mining Industry	63,400,000	1.7%
Heilingjiang Longmay Mining Group	47,890,000	1.3%
Inner Mongolia Pingzhuang Coal Industry	46,950,000	1.3%
Huolinhe Opencut Coal Industry	46,630,000	1.3%
Huadian Coal Industry	43,460,000	1.2%
Pingmei Shenma Group	40,730,000	1.1%
Yitai Group	39,340,000	1.1%
Huaibei Mining Industry	35,060,000	0.9%
Mengtai Meidian Group	32,800,000	0.9%
Inner Mongolia Huineng Meidian Group	29,420,000	0.8%
Xuzhou Coal Mining Group	28,570,000	0.8%
Guotou Coal Company	27,640,000	0.7%
Shanxi Coal Import & Export Group	23,170,000	0.6%
Shaanxi Yulin Energy Group	20,930,000	0.6%
Jilin Coal Group	20,010,000	0.5%
Huaneng Yimin Coal And Electricity Power	19,820,000	0.5%
The Rest (>7000 small producers)	1,331,100,000	35.5%

Source: CCIA (2016)

their market shares. Shenhua Group, the largest coal producer in the world, accounted for about 12% of coal production in China in 2015. The top 30 producers totally supplied about 64%, while more than 7000 small producers accounted for 36%.

Coal conversion

Unlike most Western countries, where coal is primarily used for power generation, China uses coal for a wide variety of purposes, including an entire system of coal-based chemical industry (Figure 3.3; Yang and Jackson, 2012). Almost anything that is conventionally made from oil or natural gas in other countries can also be made from coal in China. Only less than half of the coal consumed in China is for electricity (Figure 3.4).

Coal gas

Coal gas (a.k.a. town gas or manufactured gas) is a mixture of hydrogen, carbon monoxide, methane, and other volatile hydrocarbons. The exact composition of coal gas varies depending on the gasifying technique and feedstock materials. Before 1949, coal gas was only used in Shanghai and

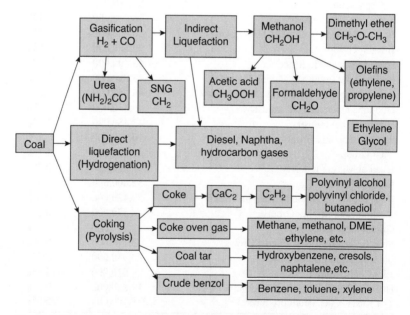

Figure 3.3 Schematic illustration of coal-derived chemicals

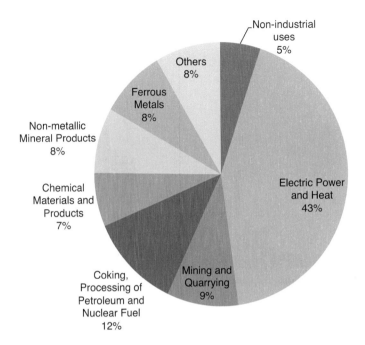

Figure 3.4 Coal consumption breakdowns in 2014

Source: NBS (2016)

several cities in Northeastern China, and all of those systems were built by foreigners. Since the 1950s, China started to build its own pipelined coal gas systems. Under the planned economy, the production of coal gas grew from 0.34 million cubic meters in 1949 to 1725 million in 1978.

In 1984, the State Council decided to ramp up urban coal gas systems to replace the inconvenient and smoky biomass and coal briquettes. The Seventh Five-Year Plan (1986–1990) stipulated that cities should actively deploy coal gas. By 1994, 147 cities had pipelined coal gas supplies. Coal gas continued to be a more popular cooking fuel than natural gas and liquefied petroleum gas (LPG) throughout the 1990s.

Coal gas production continued to grow throughout the 1990s and up to 2009. During the mid- to late 2000s, some cities started to convert coal gas networks to deliver natural gas. Natural gas is superior to coal gas because it has higher energy content and does not contain poisonous carbon monoxide. Beijing completed its transition from coal gas to natural gas in 2006. Shanghai completed its conversion in 2015. With the progress of the conversion

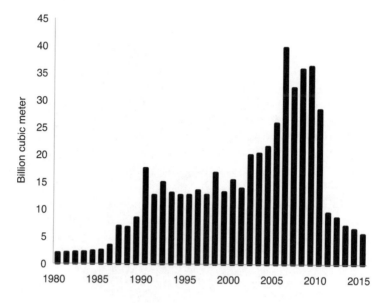

Figure 3.5 Annual supply of coal gas

Source: MOHURD (2016)

from coal gas to natural gas, the supply of coal gas has declined quickly since 2010 (Figure 3.5).

Coal-to-methanol

The first pilot project for methanol vehicles in China was initiated by the Sino-American Scientific Collaboration in 1995. The Chinese government continued to promote methanol automobiles from 1998 to 2008. However, the central government discontinued subsidies for methanol engine conversion and downgraded methanol vehicle pilot projects from national programs to provincial initiatives after 2008 (Kostka and Hobbs, 2010).

Nevertheless, several provincial governments continue to support methanol development and have stipulated methanol gasoline blending standards locally. Despite the discontinued national support, methanol industries continued to develop with provincial and local supports.

Methanol is a very versatile chemical building block and the third largest commodity (after ethylene and propylene) in the global chemical industry. It is used to make formaldehyde, methyl tertiary butyl ether (MTBE), acetic acid, dimethyl ether, esters, and olefins, and may be potentially turned into long list of other chemical products. Methanol and its derivatives are used as fuels, pesticides, medicines, lubricants, plastics, and for numerous other purposes. Almost everything that is made from crude oil or natural gas may also be made from methanol. The buildup of coal-to-methanol capacity has enabled China to substitute crude oil and nature gas with coal.

China's methanol production grew from less than 2 million metric tons in 2000 to more than 39 million in 2015. The methanol industry in China is unique in its choice of feedstock. Except for China, all other countries use natural gas to produce methanol. The carbon footprint of coal-based methanol is about three times of those made from natural gas. China is the only country that uses coal to make methanol. Roughly 84% of China's methanol output is made from coal. China has become the world's largest methanol producer and consumer. In 2015, China's methanol consumption was about 45 million metric tons, which accounted for 54% of global demand (IHS, 2017).

New coal chemicals

In China, the term "new coal chemicals" or "modern coal chemicals" refers to a group of coal conversion technologies that typically include synthetic natural gas, coal-to-liquids, and coal-to-olefins. Coal-to-methanol, coal-derived nitrogen fertilizers, and a series of other coal-derived chemicals including dimethyl ether, formaldehyde, and acetic acid are more established and often referred to as conventional coal chemicals in China. The new coal chemicals are often described as "low-carbon, highly efficient clean coal technologies" in the Chinese media and government documents.

Synthetic natural gas

Synthetic natural gas (SNG) is methane gas made from coal. The SNG technology is far more complex than coal gas and requires high capital investment. Since 2005, many Chinese companies have expressed great interests in building SNG plants and submitted proposals for government approval. The windfall profits from rising coal prices likely have enabled the coal companies to pursue risky investment. However, the central government was not supportive of SNG, due to the concern for high coal price and the potential competition for coal resources. In 2010, the National Energy Administration (NEA) issued a notice to centralize the approval of SNG projects, and forbid local governments from approving SNG projects. The NEA, nevertheless, approved four SNG demonstration projects in 2010.

At the end of 2011, coal price collapsed. With no more worries about coal price hikes, Chinese policymakers became more accommodating to alternative uses of coal. In 2012, the National Energy Administration announced 15 coal deep processing demonstration projects, which included 6 SNG plants. The development of SNG became a key focus in national coal policy agenda. The business interests in SNG continued to rise with falling coal prices throughout 2012 and 2013. By 2013, the central government has approved 9 large-scale SNG plants, with a total capacity of 37.1 billion cubic meters per year. Chinese media have described the surge of SNG and other coal conversion projects as coal chemical frenzy. Many researchers warned against the exuberance in coal conversion (Tang, 2011).

The first SNG demonstration plant, the Datang SNG project at Chifeng, Hexigten, Inner Mongolia, was completed and started production in December 2013. After merely one month of operation, in January 2014, the operators detected severe corrosion of the gasifiers and suspended production for more than two months for repairs. Meanwhile, the Datang SNG plant has also encountered difficulties in wastewater treatment, which require additional investment.

The cumulative investment of the Datang SNG plant eventually turned out to be several times higher than the original estimate. Because of the heavy financial losses in this project and others in coal chemicals, Datang Power, the owner of this project, announced its intention to divest all its investments in coal chemicals in July 2014 and entered into a framework agreement with the China Reform Holding Corporation for the restructure. Unfortunately, no one seemed to be willing to take over these nonperforming assets, and the China Reform Holding Corporation terminated the agreement in April 2016. Finally, in July 2016, Datang Power sold its entire coal chemical assets for the symbolic price of 1 RMB (about US\$0.15) to another company within the Datang Group. Over the course its coal chemical venture, Datang Power invested more than 60 billion RMB, but eventually sold them for 1 RMB. The sale is indeed a euphemism for bankruptcy.

The 12th Five-Year Plan (2011–2015) for Natural Gas Development planned for the total annual SNG production to reach 15–18 billion cubic meters by 2015 and 60 billion by 2020. However, after the oil and gas price collapse in 2014, the outlook for SNG suddenly turned gloomy. The investment enthusiasm quickly dwindled. The actual SNG output in 2015 was only about 1.6 billion cubic meters (CNEnergy, 2016).

SNG has a very high carbon footprint. The life-cycle CO_2 emissions of SNG are roughly three times as much as that of regular natural gas (Yang, 2016). China is the only country that is actively developing this very high-carbon technology.

Coal-to-liquids

Inspired by the South African experiences in making gasoline and diesel from coal, Chinese policymakers have long been interested in developing coal-to-liquids industry. Nevertheless, during the coal chemical frenzy in the early 2000s, the central government was cautious.

China Shenhua Coal to Liquid and Chemical Company started to build its first coal-to-liquid plant in 2004 and completed it in 2008. In 2008, the NDRC ordered the suspension of all coal-to-liquids projects, except for the two by Shenhua Group, which included the already completed direct liquefaction plant in Ordos, Inner Mongolia, and the proposed indirect liquefaction project in Ningxia. In 2012, the central government approved another coal-to-liquids project, a joint venture by Yangquan Coal Industry and Yanchang Petroleum Company.

The low oil prices since 2014 have made coal-to-liquids uncompetitive. However, the projects that were already under construction have little choice but to continue. By 2015, the total installed capacity of coal-to-liquids reached 2.78 million metric tons per year, but the capacity utilization was very low. The actual coal-to-liquids output in 2015 was 1.32 million metric tons (CNEnergy, 2016).

Coal-to-olefins

Coal-to-olefins mainly targets producing ethylene and propylene, which are the most important and versatile commodities in the chemical industry. Globally, the most dominant feedstock for manufacturing olefins is naphtha, accounting for roughly half of the global output of olefins, followed by ethane and propane. Coal-to-olefins is more expensive and dirtier (more toxic wastewater and seven to nine times more CO_2 emissions) than olefins from other feedstock (Yang, 2016). China is the only country that uses coal to make olefins.

The first coal-to-olefins plant was completed in 2010. Since then, the capacity has been expanding quickly, from almost zero before 2010 to about 7.9 million metric ton per year by the end of 2015. Many more have been planned.

Environmental violations of clean coal

Despite being promoted as clean coal technology, the modern coal chemicals industry in China has a rather infamous environmental record. In 2013, Greenpeace released an investigation report on the illegal groundwater withdraw by the Shenhua coal-to-liquid plant (Greenpeace, 2013). Datang Doulun coal-based methanol-to-propylene plant was caught multiple times by the Doulun county environmental bureau for illegal dumping of toxic wastewater, leakage of evaporation pond, groundwater contamination, and air pollution.

In 2014, Greenpeace released another investigation report on the environmental violations of the Datang SNG plant. In 2016, China Central TV station aired a special news episode on the repeated environmental violations of the Yunnan Xianfeng Chemical Industry, which produce methanol, gasoline, and SNG from lignite (CCTV, 2016). While Chinese government officials sometimes acknowledge the environmental problems of coal chemicals, they typically justify the continued support for coal chemicals on the basis of energy security.

Chapter highlights

- The coal industry in China is fragmented and competitive.
- The Chinese government continues to intervene in the coal market after price decontrol.
- China uses coal for a wide range of purposes. Power generation accounted only for less than half of coal consumption in China.
- Coal conversion industries, which are highly polluting and with extremely high carbon footprints, are promoted in China as clean coal technology.

References

Andrews-Speed, P., Yang, M., Shen, L., Cao, S., 2003. The regulation of China's township and village coal mines: A study of complexity and ineffectiveness. *Journal of Cleaner Production* 11, 185–196

Barboza, D., 2010. A new Chinese city, with everything but people. *New York Times*, November 19

BBC, 2012. Ordos: The biggest ghost town in China. *BBC News*, March 17

BP, 2016. *Statistical Review of World Energy*. BP, London

Cao, X., 2008. *Legal Institutions of China's Small Mines From the Perspective of Sustainable Development*. China Financial and Economic Publishing House, Beijing (in Chinese: 曹霞, 2008. 可持续发展视野下中国小矿的法律规制. 中国财政经济出版社)

CCIA, 2016. *2015 Top 50 Coal Producers in China*. China Coal Industry Association. www.coalchina.org.cn/detail/16/09/05/00000037/content.html (in Chinese) (accessed 1/04/2017)

CCTV, 2016. *Pollution 'Pioneer' Poisoned Yunnan*. http://tv.cctv.com/2016/12/05/ VIDEM3B761cZI4R89hh0P9VH161205.shtml (in Chinese) (accessed 12/12/2016)

CNEnergy, 2016. *2016 Petroleum Industry Capacity Warning Report*. www.cnenergy. org/yq/lh/201604/t20160413_276757.html (in Chinese) (accessed 12/12/2016)

Economic Daily, 2016. *Statistics Show that By the End of 2015 National Total Scale of Coal Mining Was 5.7 Billion Tonnes*. www.ce.cn/xwzx/gnsz/gdxw/201601/12/ t20160112_8209550.shtml (in Chinese) (accessed 12/09/2016)

Exbulk, 2017. www.exbulk.com/list-78-1.html (in Chinese) (accessed 1/4/2017)

Greenpeace, 2013. *Thirsty Coal 2: Shenhua's Water Grab* www.greenpeace. org/eastasia/publications/reports/climate-energy/2013/thirsty-coal-two-china/ (accessed 3/18/2017)

IHS, 2017. *China Dominates Global Methanol Capacity and Demand*. http://news. ihsmarkit.com/press-release/country-industry-forecasting-media/china-dominates-global-methanol-capacity-and-demand (accessed 2/16/2017)

IMF, 2016. *Primary Commodity Prices*. Washington, DC: International Monetary Fund

Kostka, G., Hobbs, W., 2010. *Embedded Interests and the Managerial Local State: Methanol Fuel-Switching in China*. Frankfurt: Frankfurt School of Finance & Management

Li, Y., 2007. *Firmly Rely on Local Party Secretary and Government to Resolutely Rectify and Close Down Coal Mines*. www.chinasafety.gov.cn/zhengwugong-kai/2007-06/05/content_243349.htm (in Chinese) (accessed 12/09/2016)

MOHURD, 2016. *China Urban-Rural Construction Statistical Yearbook 2015*. Ministry of Housing and Urban-Rural Development, Beijing. www.mohurd.gov.cn/ xytj/tjzljsxytjgb/jstjnj/index.html (in Chinese) (accessed 1/7/2017)

NBS, 2002. *2001 Statistical Report on National Economic and Social Development*. National Bureau of Statistics, Beijing (in Chinese: 2001年国民经济和社会发展 统计公报)

NBS, 2010. *China Compendium of Statistics 1940–2008*. National Bureau of Statistics/China Statistics Press, Beijing

NBS, 2016. *China Energy Statistical Yearbook*. National Bureau of Statistics of China. http://data.stats.gov.cn/ (accessed 1/4/2017)

NDRC, 2016. *Notice on Further Regulating and Improving Coal Production and Operation Orders*. www.sdpc.gov.cn/gzdt/201605/t20160518_802085.html (in Chinese) (accessed 1/10/2017)

Peng, L., 2005. *The First Decade of Internet Media in China*. Tsinghua University Press, Beijing (in Chinese: 彭兰, 中国网络媒体的第一个十年. 清华大学出版社)

Shanghai Securities News, 2016. *NDRC Is Very Concerned; Warning Coal Industries to Regulate their Prices*. http://energy.people.com.cn/n1/2016/1104/c71661-28834310.html (in Chinese) (accessed 12/09/2016)

State Council, 2016. *State Council's Opinions to Resolve Overcapacity Problem of Coal Industry*. www.gov.cn/zhengce/content/2016-02/05/content_5039686.htm (in Chinese) (accessed 1/10/2017)

Tang, H.-Q., 2011. Six turns of enthusiasm waves in coal chemical industry development. *Chemical Engineering Design Communications* (in Chinese) 37, 1–9 (in Chinese: 唐宏青, 煤化工的6轮热潮,化工设计通讯)

VOC, 2016. http://hunan.voc.com.cn/article/201603/201603240814078103.html (in Chinese) (accessed 12/11/2016)

Wang, B., 2014. *The NDRC Hosted 18 Coordination Meetings; Big Rescue for 300 Million Tonnes of Coal Inventories.* www.chinatimes.cc/article/46052.html (in Chinese) (accessed 12/08/2016)

Yang, C.-J., 2016. Coal chemicals: China's high-carbon clean coal programme? *Climate Policy* 16, 1–6

Yang, C.-J., Jackson, R.B., 2012. China's growing methanol economy and its implications for energy and the environment. *Energy Policy* 41, 878–884

Yang, C.-J., Xuan, X., Jackson, R.B., 2012. China's coal price disturbances: Observations, explanations, and implications for global energy economies. *Energy Policy* 51, 720–727

4   Oil and gas

China's oil consumption has increased by more than 4,000 times from 1949 to 2015. Since 2003, China has become the second largest oil consuming country in the world. The three Chinese national oil corporations ranked the 3rd, 4th, and 109th in the Fortune Global 500 list in 2016. The Chinese oil companies have become increasingly active in the international markets.

Contrary to the coal industry, China's oil and gas industry has always been highly centralized. Ever since the People's Republic of China was established in 1949, the exploration and production of oil has always been a top priority in the national policy agenda. During the Cultural Revolution, the Daqing oilfield was a prominent symbol in Chinese Communist propaganda. Over time, petroleum technocrats formed the oil clique and became a powerful faction in Chinese politics.

Evolution of the oil industry

Before 1982, all oil and gas exploration and production activities in China were organized by a ministry in the central government, although the ministry was restructured and renamed many times (Table 4.1).

In 1950, the Ministry of Fuel Industry has started oil exploration in Sichuan basin and geological survey in the Ordos basin. In 1952, the People's Liberation Army (PLA) reorganized its 57th division and renamed it as the first division of petroleum engineering. The PLA provided important workforces in the exploration and production of oil and gas in the command economy. The exploration activities predominantly aimed for oil, although sometimes they found natural gas instead or as a by-product.

In 1954, a team led by Soviet geologist P. I. Uvalov discovered the Karamay oilfield, which soon became the largest oilfield in China in the 1950s (Kraus, 2010). The even bigger Daqing oilfield in Heilongjiang was found in 1959. A few small oilfields were found in Qinghai and Sichuan.

Table 4.1 Ministry in charge of oil and gas from 1949 to 1988

Period	Ministry in charge of oil and gas
1949–1955	Ministry of Fuel Industry
1955–1970	Ministry of Petroleum Industry
1970–1975	Ministry of Fuel and Chemical Industry
1975–1978	Ministry of Petrochemical Industry
1978–1988	Ministry of Petroleum Industry

After the Sino-Soviet split in 1960, not only did China lose Soviet assistance; Mao Zedong also started to perceive military threat from every direction: the Soviet Union on the north and west, the United States and Taiwan on the east, and India on the south (Lieberthal and Oksenberg, 1988). In order to prepare for the perceived imminent military conflicts, China urgently needed to increase its oil supply.

Under the policy of self-reliance, China actively developed its oilfields in the 1960s with national planning and massive mobilization of labor. In 1960, the People's Liberation Army transferred 30,000 personnel to the Ministry of Petroleum Industry to support the development of Daqing oilfield. Communist leaders called on the soldiers' patriotism and dedication to Mao Zedong to motivate them under harsh working conditions.

The successful production at Daqing oilfield soon became the most prominent showcase in the Chinese Communist propaganda. The Daqing experience was promoted as the epitome of Maoist doctrine of industrialization (Figure 4.1). Chinese propaganda channels advertised the stories of Daqing and included them in school curriculums. The legendary status of Daqing also elevated the political status of petroleum technocrats, which marked the beginning of the oil clique (Page et al., 2013).

Another major oilfield, Shengli oilfield, was discovered in 1961 and soon became China's second largest oilfield. In December 1963, at National People's Congress, Premier Zhou Enlai declared that China had become self-sufficient in oil, and that Chinese people would never use foreign oil again.

In the 1960s, China started to export oil in small amount and used the acquired foreign currency to buy industrial equipment from Japan and Europe. The oil export gradually increased over time. By the 1970s, oil export had become China's major source of foreign currency. The exploration and production of oil remained a top priority in China's economic plans. Throughout the 1970s, China's oil production increased very rapidly. China remained a net oil exporter until 1992.

The Oil Crisis of 1973 was a blessing for China. During the Oil Crisis, China rapidly increased its oil exports, mainly to Japan and the Philippines.

Figure 4.1 Propaganda poster of Daqing

("Study the revolutionary spirit of Daqing, hold high the great red banner of Mao Zedong Thought, to struggle for the realization of the Third Five-Year Plan!")

Source: IISH/Stefan R. Landsberger Collections. Courtesy of chineseposter.net

Throughout the Cultural Revolution (1966–1976), the standards of living in China remained low. The Chinese government used the increased revenues from oil export mainly on industrialization, military expenditure, and foreign aids. In particular, China provided US$20 billion worth of military aid to North Vietnam during its war against the Americans (Xi et al., 2015).

Several oilfields were near depletion by late 1970s, and oil outputs declined from 1979 to 1981 (Figure 4.2). In December 1979, the drillship "Bohai No. 2" capsized and sank, resulting in 72 deaths. This event was the worst accident in the history of China's oil industry. Vice Premier Kang Shi'en, who was in charge of energy, was reprimanded. The Minister of Petroleum Industry resigned, and several senior officials were sentenced to jail. This event demoralized the oil technocrat group, and some Chinese articles indicated that the demoralized oil personnel contributed to the reduced oil production in 1980–1981 (Fang, 2013; Wei, 2015). In order to restore the morale and revive the oil industry, Kagn Shi'en was reinstalled as the Minister of Petroleum Industry in 1982. This incident showed that the oil clique had become an influential force within the Chinese government.

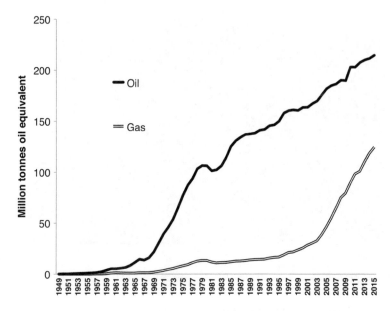

Figure 4.2 Oil and gas production in China
Source: NBS (2010); BP (2016)

At that time, the oil industry was organized as a government bureau, where workers were government employees. During the Cultural Revolution, propaganda and political campaigns were the primary modes of worker motivation. After the economic reform in 1978, policymakers started to reconsider the institutional design and incentive scheme for the oil industry.

In the early 1980s, Chinese policymakers decided that the oil industry was better organized as a business and started to separate it from government administration. Three national oil companies were established. China National Offshore Oil Corporation (CNOOC) was established in 1982 to be responsible for all offshore oil and gas production. In 1983, the Ministry of Petroleum Industry separated its assets in refinery and petrochemical production and spun them off as China Petrochemical Corporation Group (Sinopec Group). Finally, in 1988, the remaining assets (mainly in onshore oil and gas exploration and production) were reorganized as the China National Petroleum Corporation (CNPC/PetroChina), and the Ministry of Petroleum Industry was abolished in the same year.

The three national oil corporations were mainly divided according to their different functions with limited overlaps. The design was clearly not to encourage competition. Nevertheless, over time, the three national oil companies have gradually ventured into each other's domain and competed against each other in some areas.

Oil pricing reform

Before the early 1980s, Chinese government administration set the oil price at a fixed level. The oil price remained unchanged for 20 years. In 1981, the dual-track system was applied to the oil industry. The State Council charged the Ministry of Petroleum Industry (MPI) with the quota of 100 million metric tons and permitted the MPI to sell its above-plan output at international price. The MPI was allowed to keep the revenue from oil export. The MPI broke down the national quota and assigned a quota to each oilfield. Oil workers and managers could earn bonuses from the above-quota revenues. The financial incentives effectively motivated oil workers. China's oil production started to increase again after the 1979–1981 declines (Figure 4.2).

China has maintained domestic oil price control until today. However, the practice of price control has become more flexible over time. Before 1998, the Chinese government kept the domestic oil price much lower than international prices. The controlled domestic oil price typically was kept at a constant level for years.

China became a net oil importer in 1993, and gradually increased its imports over time. The national oil companies were responsible for buying oil in the international markets and supply to the domestic markets at controlled low price. Of course, buy high and sell low is never a good business model. Within a few years, it has become clear that such practice was not financially sustainable.

In 1998, the State Planning Commission announced its oil price reform plan, which authorized PetroChina and Sinopec to negotiate the prices of domestically produced crude oil, and established the principle that domestic gasoline and diesel prices should be in line with international prices. Starting in June 2000, the controlled domestic oil prices became pegged to the market price in Singapore. In November 2001, the controlled pricing scheme was revised to be pegged to weighted average of market prices in New York, Rotterdam, and Singapore.

Technically speaking, China has never relinquished its oil price control. However, by pegging its controlled prices to international market prices, the oil prices in China have become essentially market-driven. Figure 4.3 compares the retailed gasoline prices in China and the United States. It shows that the adjustments of controlled oil prices in China have become increasingly frequent, and the movements are largely consistent with international market prices. The controlled gasoline prices in China were much lower than the average market prices in the United States before 2009, and became

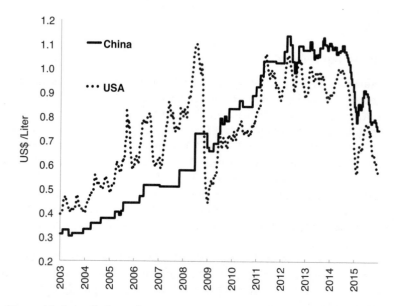

Figure 4.3 Controlled gasoline prices in China versus average market gasoline prices in the United States

Source: Reuters (2012); Reuters (2016); USEIA (2016)

higher after 2009. The changed pricing practice significantly improved the national oil companies' finance.

Natural gas pricing reform

Natural gas has always been a sideline sector in the petroleum industry. The Chinese government devoted little resource to explore natural gas. As a result, the growth of natural gas production was much slower than oil until the early 2000s (Figure 4.2).

From 1949 to 1987, the government set a single wellhead price for all natural gas in China. The controlled wellhead price was adjusted only seven times during this period. The dual-track pricing system for natural gas started in 1978. Unlike dual-track pricing for most other commodities, where producers were allowed to sell their above-plan output at market prices, the natural gas dual-track pricing did not allow free market prices. The above-plan outputs received a higher but still government-set price.

Even the higher above-plan price was still much lower than the prevailing market price of natural gas in East Asia. Low controlled price and low priority in national policy agenda discouraged the development of natural gas in China for more than half a century (Yang et al., 2014).

In 1992, the State Planning Commission implemented a more complex pricing scheme for natural gas. The pricing differed not only according to whether it is within a planned quota, but also the purpose of use (fertilizer, residential, commercial, and industrial). These prices continued to be much lower than those in the neighboring East Asian countries.

Before 2005, natural gas prices were only adjusted once every several years (in 1992, 1994, 1997, 2002, and 2005). The prices remained constant between the adjustments. With each adjustment, the pricing scheme became increasingly complex. The prices not only differed due to plan or above-plan and user categories, but also according to which gas field it came from. Meanwhile, the National Development and Reform Commission (NDRC) gradually allow some flexible pricing within 10% of the government's directive prices.

Since 2005, the NDRC started to adjust natural gas prices once a year, but the controlled prices remained low. Price control discouraged both domestic production and import. As a result, natural gas shortages occurred in many Chinese cities almost every year from 2004 to 2014, and many researchers called for pricing reform to relieve the shortages (Dong et al., 2010).

China did not import any natural gas before 2006, when the first liquefied natural gas (LNG) receiving terminal in China was completed in Guangdong province. The first imported pipelined natural gas from Turkmenistan started in 2010. The national oil corporations were responsible for importing natural gas. Once again, the national corporations were compelled to buy high and sell low, and suffered financial losses. However, to the gigantic national oil corporations, the losses in natural gas imports were small compared to their revenues from oil. The smaller financial stakes before the 2010s might explain for the slow progress in natural gas pricing reform.

Many more LNG terminals were built since 2006. By the end of 2015, China already had 11 operational LNG terminals, and many more were under construction. The Sino-Myanmar natural gas pipeline was completed in 2013. The Turkmenistan-China natural gas pipeline was expanded to receive gas from Uzbekistan and Kazakhstan. Natural gas imports increased rapidly from zero before 2006 to about 30% of total consumption during 2013–2015 (Figure 4.4).

Since 2012, the natural gas pricing reforms have picked up speed. The prices for unconventional natural gas, including coal-bed methane, shale

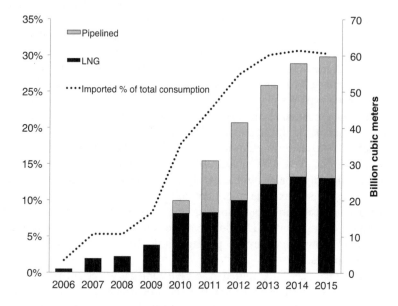

Figure 4.4 Natural gas imports in China
Source: BP (2016)

gas, and synthetic natural gas, was decontrolled in 2012, and an experimental, market-pegged pricing scheme in two coastal provinces, Guangdong and Guangxi, started. Similar to the market-pegged oil price control, the pilot program for natural gas pricing reform set the controlled prices according to the market prices of alternative fuels (fuel oil and liquefied petroleum gas). In June 2013, the NDRC extended the market-referenced pricing scheme to the incremental consumption of non-residential natural gas in 2013 (incremental gas, or new gas), while maintained traditional cost-based prices for the consumed volume in 2012 (stock gas, or old gas). The differentiation between incremental gas (new gas) and stock gas (old gas) was to minimize the price hikes to existing consumers, and impose market-referenced pricing only on new gas users. This approach was neither fair nor efficient. However, it was politically savvy because it protected the vested interests.

In 2014, the international LNG prices collapsed, and China suddenly started to experience a surplus of natural gas supply. The sudden surplus eased the political resistance to pricing reform. In 2015, the NDRC equalized the prices of stock (old) and incremental (new) gas for all non-residential users. Market-pegged pricing was extended to cover all non-residential uses of natural gas, which accounted for about 80% of total natural gas consumption in China. The prices of residential uses of natural gas remained controlled well below market level.

In October 2016, the NDRC initiated a pilot scheme of free-market prices for both residential and non-residential natural gas in Fujian province. A month later, the NDRC announced complete price decontrol of fertilizer-purposed natural gas, and started to allow the natural gas suppliers and fertilizer companies to negotiate their prices in free market (NDRC, 2016).

By the time this book is written (at the end of 2016), the natural gas price decontrol is still incomplete. A few relatively small sectors (unconventional gas, Fujiang Province, fertilizer) only recently started to experiment free market pricing. Most of the industrial users pay controlled but market-pegged prices, and most residential users enjoy controlled cost-based low prices.

Energy security

In 2015, China relied on foreign imports for about 60% of its oil consumption and 30% of natural gas. The increasingly high dependence on imported energy has become a national security concern. Chinese scholars recognize that self-sufficiency is neither practical nor wise. If China increases domestic oil and gas production, it will only accelerate their depletion and jeopardize China's long-term security.

The heavy reliance of crude oil imports on the maritime transport through the Malacca Strait is a particular concern. In 2011, about 85% of China's crude oil imports passed through the Malacca Strait (USDOD, 2012). Following the philosophy of not to put all the eggs in one basket, China developed multiple transit routes for oil and gas imports. The Kazakhstan-China oil pipeline and Turkmenistan-China gas pipeline supply energy to China from the northwest. The Russia-China oil pipeline delivers oil from Siberia to the northeast China. The Russia-China gas pipeline is expected to be completed by 2019. The Sino-Myanmar oil and gas pipelines form the southwest energy route to China. The pipelines and the maritime oil and LNG shipping (from southeast) constitute the four major energy routes (northeast, northwest, southeast, southwest). In addition, China is developing pipelines along its proposed China-Pakistan economic corridor to form a new energy route.

China started to build its strategic oil reserve in 2004. The first phase project with stockpile capacity of 14 million metric tons (equivalent to 10 days of China's oil imports) was completed in 2008. The second and third phase each is designed with 18 million metric tons of stockpile. Even after the scheduled completion of the third phase in 2020, China's strategic oil reserve will still be far below the 90-days level recommended by the International Energy Agency (IEA).

Overseas acquisitions

Chinese national companies suddenly increased their overseas acquisitions of oil and gas resources since 2009 (Figure 4.5). The timing coincided with the changed domestic gasoline and diesel pricing practice in 2009 (Figure 4.3), which increased the financial resources available to the national oil companies.

Many foreign commentators were suspicious of China's intention in the sudden increase of overseas acquisitions. An investigation by the International Energy Agency, however, found no evidence linking the overseas activities to China's energy security strategy, and concluded that these activities were mainly driven by commercial incentives (Liang and Sinton, 2011).

Before 2011, the equity shares of Chinese oil companies' foreign assets were highly concentrated in Kazakhstan, Sudan, Venezuela, and Angola. After suffering heavy losses in socioeconomic crises in some politically unstable

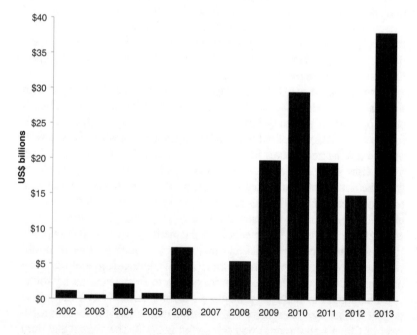

Figure 4.5 Chinese overseas oil and gas acquisitions

Source: Liang and Sinton (2011); Liang and Ding (2014)

countries, Chinese investments started to move toward areas with more stable political environment after 2011. The experiences in Sudan, Venezuela, and Angola were likely the most traumatic for China.

Sudan

CNPC was the largest foreign investor in both Sudan and South Sudan, when the South seceded in 2011. In 2012, Sudan shut down the oil pipeline from South Sudan due to disputes over fees. South Sudan soon shut down all oil production throughout the country and expelled the Chinese chief of oil operation. The shutdown continued for over a year and caused enormous economic damages and social turmoil in both countries. In 2013, a civil war broke out in South Sudan. The violent conflicts in Sudan and South Sudan inflicted huge losses on CNPC.

Venezuela

CNPC started to invest in Venezuela as early as 1997. The amounts of investment remained modest until 2007, when China provided US$4 billion to establish the Joint Chinese-Venezuelan Fund. The fund was mainly operated according to the "loan for oil" principle (i.e., Venezuela will pay back its debt by shipping oil to China). China provided additional loans almost every year since 2007. After the oil price collapse in 2014, Venezuela suffered severe fiscal shortage, which turned into economic crisis. China provided additional loans in 2014 and 2015, and loosened the terms of its existing loans. Unfortunately, the Chinese assistance was not able to reverse the dire situation in Venezuela. According to an estimate by a NDRC official (Fang, 2015), the total Chinese loans to Venezuela amounted to US$56 billion by 2016. After deducting the value of delivered oil, Venezuela still owes China about US$20 billion. By the time this book is written, it is not yet clear whether China will continue to throw money into the failing state, or to cut its losses at some point.

Angola

In 2004, Sinopec acquired an offshore oilfield in Angola, through the brokerage of Sam Pa, the head of the China International Fund (CIF), a private company registered in Hong Kong (Morrissey et al., 2011). With the assistance of CIF and its subsidiary China-Sonangol, Sinopec acquired many oilfields in Angola from 2004 to 2007. In 2007, the president of Sinopec, Chen Tonghai, stepped down with charges of corruption, and was later found guilty and sentenced to death in 2009. After Chen stepped down, Su Shulin succeeded as the head of Sinopec. Under the new leadership, Sinopec continued to partner with CIF and China-Sonangol in acquiring more oil assets in Angola, and gradually expanded their scope to other African countries. In many cases, Sinopec won the biddings with surprisingly high prices (Wang, 2015).

In 2015, Su Shulin was arrested for corruption charges about the Sinopec investments in Angola, which included the purchase of many intentionally overpriced oilfields. Sam Pa was also arrested for related charged. Sinopec suffered heavy losses from corruption and mismanaged overseas activities (Huang et al., 2015).

Overseas acquisitions provided plenty opportunities for corruption. Bo Qiliang, the head of CNPC overseas operation, was investigated for corruption and arrested in 2014. The State-owned Assets Supervision and Administration Commission later named Bo Qiliang and its CNPC overseas activities as the most corrupted management in China's state-owned companies (Shiyoutz, 2015). In a way, the oil oligarchy siphoned money out of Chinese consumers' wallets, squandered it overseas, and enriched their private pockets in the process.

Political infighting over fuel quality standards

The power of the oil clique and the national oil companies was also manifested in their fights against the Ministry of Environmental Protection over the automotive fuel quality standards.

In order to control the worsening urban air qualities, China adopted the Euro 1 standard and enacted its first vehicle emission standard in 2000. However, the automotive emission control technologies cannot function properly without the fuels of sufficiently low impurities. China's national environmental authority was in charge of the vehicle emission standards, but not the automotive fuel quality standards. The jurisdiction of fuel quality falls into the National Petroleum Products and Lubricants Standardized Technology Committee, which was dominated by personnel from the national oil companies.

Because the upgrades of fuel quality require expensive investments at refineries, the national oil companies are incentivized to resist and delay tougher standards. For years, fuel quality has remained a major bottleneck to improving China's urban air quality (Yang et al., 2015). In China, fuel quality upgrades always lag behind vehicle upgrades.

Numerous news reports and expert testimonies have blamed the national oil companies for resisting changes to reduce pollution. In 2015, Chai Jin, a former China Central Television journalist, released a high-impact documentary on China's air pollution, where she also pointed to the cartel of the national oil companies as a major obstacle in cleaning China's air.

Oil clique

Over time, the oil clique evolved into a major faction in the Chinese Communist Party and expanded its sphere of influence beyond the oil industry. During the early years of Chinese economic reform, the oil clique sided with the conservatives against the reformists. During the Hu Jintao Administration (2003–2012), Zeng Qinghong, the leader of the oil clique, served as the Vice President of China and promoted many officials from the oil clique. National economic policies during this period were generally in favor of the national oil companies. A common Chinese phrase "guo jin min tui," meaning that the state advanced and the private sector retreated, was frequently used to described the economic development in this period (Weatley, 2009).

After President Xi Jinping assumed office in 2012, he initiated a large anti-corruption campaign. The crackdown on the oil clique was a major part of the anti-corruption investigation. In 2013, Jiang Jiemin, director of the State-owned Assets Supervision and Administration Commission and former chairman of CNPC, was arrested and later sentenced to prison. The crackdown on the oil clique was considered more than just about corruption, but also a momentous step in Xi's consolidation of power (Buckley, 2013). The demise of the oil clique could have long-lasting impacts on the future of China's energy policy and politics. However, it is not yet clear what the exact implications will be.

Chapter highlights

- The Chinese oil and gas industry is highly concentrated. The three national oil companies dominate the market.
- Oil and gas prices in China remained controlled until today, but the practices of control have become increasingly flexible over time.
- China has been building multiple routes of oil and gas imports to enhance its long-term energy security, but its strategic petroleum reserve for short-term emergency has remained grossly inadequate.
- Historically, the oil clique has enjoyed great influences in Chinese government. The fall of the oil clique will likely have long-term implications on not only energy policy but also the overall Chinese politics.

References

BP, 2016. *Statistical Review of World Energy*. BP, London

Buckley, C., 2013. Political test in China as corruption probe encircles an oil titan. *The New York Times*, September 15. http://cn.nytimes.com/china/20130925/c25corruption/en-us/ (accessed 12/17/2016)

44 Oil and gas

Dong, X., Tong, J., Li, J., 2010. A brief analysis of China's natural gas reform. *Sino-Global Energy* 15, 6–10 (in Chinese: 董秀成, 佟金辉, 李君臣, 我国天然气价格改革浅析,中外能源)

Fang, S., 2015. Current state of Venezuelan inflation crisis and prospect for China-Venezuela relation. *China Economic and Trade Herald* 22, 50–52 (in Chinese: 苑生龙, 委内瑞拉通涨危机现状及中委关系展望, 中国经贸导刊)

Fang, Z., 2013. *Reality of 'Bohai 2' Sinking.* China Petroleum. www.chinacpc.com. cn/info/2013-12-25/news_286.html (in Chinese) (accessed 12/14/2016)

Huang, K., Wang, X., Yu, N., 2015. Auditors probe Sinopec, Savvy Broker in Angola. *Caixin,* August 4. http://english.caixin.com/2015-08-04/100836237.html (accessed 12/18/2016)

Kraus, C., 2010. Creating a Soviet 'semi-colony'? Sino-Soviet cooperation and its demise in Xinjiang, 1949–1955. *The Chinese Historical Review* 17, 129–165

Liang, J., Ding, C., 2014. *Update on Overseas Investments by Chinese National Oil Companies.* International Energy Agency, Paris

Liang, J., Sinton, J., 2011. *Overseas Investments by Chinese National Oil Companies.* International Energy Agency, Paris

Lieberthal, K., Oksenberg, M., 1988. Policy *Making in China: Leaders, Structures, and Processes.* Princeton University Press. Princeton, NJ

Morrissey, B., Ojha, H., Murray, L.R., Martin-Menard, P., 2011. *China-based Corporate Web Behind Troubled Africa Resource Deals.* www.publicintegrity. org/2011/11/09/7108/china-based-corporate-web-behind-troubled-africa-resource-deals (accessed 12/18/2016)

NBS, 2010. *China Compendium of Statistics 1949–2008.* National Bureau of Statistics, Beijing (in Chinese: 新中国60年统计资料汇编)

NDRC, 2016. *Notice on Market Reform of Natural Gas Price for Chemical Fertilizer.* www.ndrc.gov.cn/zcfb/zcfbtz/201611/t20161110_826163.html (in Chinese) (accessed 12/15/2016)

Page, J., Spegele, B., Ma, W., 2013. Powerful oil clique at center of Chinese probes. *Wall Street Journal,* September 5

Reuters, 2012. Table-China retail gasoline, diesel prices since 2003. *Reuters,* March 19. www.reuters.com/article/2012/03/19/china-fuel-prices-idUSL3E8EJ8LJ20120319 (accessed 12/18/2016)

Reuters, 2016. China retail gasoline, diesel price adjustments since 2014. *Reuters,* December 14. http://cn.reuters.com/article/idCNL4S1E930E (in Chinese) (accessed 1/4/2017)

Shiyoutz, 2015. *State Asset Supervisory Commission Report Reveals Five Largest Losses of Assets; PetroChina Bo Quliang Listed.* www.shiyoutz.com/pinglun/29491. html (in Chinese) (accessed 12/17/2016)

USDOD, 2012. *Annual Report to Congress: Military and Security Development Involving the People's Republic of China 2012.* U.S. Department of Defense

USEIA, 2016. *Weekly U.S. All Grades All Formulations Retail Gasoline Prices.* U.S. Energy Information Administration

Wang, Z., 2015. *Shi Jinghua Trap Chinese Companies; China International Fund Siphoned Money From Africa.* http://money.163.com/special/view617/ (in Chinese) (accessed 12/18/2016)

Weatley, A., 2009. Analysis – In China's economy as elsewhere, the state rises. *Reuters*, March 16. http://in.reuters.com/article/idININdia-38523620090316 (accessed 12/17/2016)

Wei, R., 2015. *Memory of China's Oil Output Reduction in 1980*. http://oilobserver. com/history/article/1438 (in Chinese) (accessed 12/14/2016)

Xi, L., Ti, T., Cai, X., 2015. World oil crisis and the strategic development of China's oil trade. *Researches in Chinese Economic History* 5, 136–142 (in Chinese: 习莉 邰婷婷蔡翔世界石油危机与中国石油贸易的战略发展(1973–1998) 中国经济 史研究, 2015年第5期)

Yang, C.-J., Zhou, Y., Jackson, R.B., 2014. China's fuel gas sector: History, current status, and future prospects. *Utilities Policy* 28, 12–21

Yang, Z., Wang, H., Shao, Z., Muncrief, R., 2015. *Review of Beijing's Comprehensive Motor Vehicle Emission Control Programs*. The International Council on Clean Transportation

5 Electricity

China surpassed the United States in electric power generation and consumption as of 2011. The State Grid Corporation of China (SGCC) is now the largest electric utility company in the world. The 2015 revenue of SGCC was US$329.6 billion, roughly 14 times of the 2015 revenue (US$23.5 billion) of Duke Energy, the largest electric utility in the United States. China's enormous electric power industry started from an extremely small basis more than six decades ago. From 1949 to 2015, annual power generation in China increased by more than a thousand times, from 4.3 to 5740 terawatts-hours (CEC, 2016).

Before 1997, a ministry in the central government was responsible for power generation. It looks like the Chinese government could not make up its mind about what to call this ministry (Table 5.1). Despite the back-and-forth, power generation gradually increased under direct government control.

Electric power in the planned economy

From 1949 to 1952, the Ministry of Fuel Industry organized the repairs and reinstallation of war-torn power facilities (Yang, 2008a). During the First Five-Year Plan (1953–1958), 23 coal-fired thermal power plants and one

Table 5.1 Ministry in charge of electric power

1949–1955	Ministry of Fuel Industry
1955–1958	Ministry of Electric Power Industry
1958–1979	Ministry of Water Resources and Electric Power
1979–1982	Ministry of Electric Power Industry
1982–1988	Ministry of Water Resources and Electric Power
1993–1998	Ministry of Electric Power Industry

hydropower station were built. Several thermal power equipment manufacturing bases in Harbin and Shanghai were also established with technology transfers from Czech and the Soviet Union. At that time, Chinese economic planners prioritized coal-fired power over hydropower because thermal power plants were cheaper and faster to build.

During the Great Leap Forward, the electric power sector was not immune to the political frenzy. The races to build too many power plants led to poor design and hastened installations. The existing generators were encouraged to operate as much above their designed rating as possible. As a result, there were numerous incidents of boiler explosions, broken turbine blades, burnt generators, and other damages (Yang, 2008b). In 1961, in light of the damage caused by the Great Leap Forward, the central government changed its policy to stop building new power plants, and suspend and postpone existing power plant projects for repairs.

After the Sino-Soviet split in 1960, China pursued the policy of self-reliance and the "Third Front" (1964–1975) strategy to prepare for war. According to the "Third Front" strategy, many industries were moved to the inland provinces so they will be safe from foreign invasions. An important guiding principle was to build many small distributed thermal power plants in caves or near mountains for military defense. Many of these power plants in caves were quickly damaged by high humidity and had to be abandoned or removed. The Third Front policy caused huge financial losses in the end.

Under the planned economy, the purpose of power generation was mainly to serve the industry and the cities. Rural electrification was relatively neglected. By 1978, about half of Chinese citizens (450 million) still had no electricity at all (Wang, 2013). After the 1978 economic reform, the Chinese government started to pay more attention to rural electrification.

Rural electrification

In 1982, the Ministry of Water Resources and Electric Power initiated a pilot program of rural electrification in 100 counties. The development of small hydropower was particularly emphasized. After the successful electrification of the first 100 counties, the program proceeded to electrify another 200 counties in the Eighth Five-Year Plan (1991–1995). The rural electrification pilot programs successfully expanded the coverage of electricity services. By 1997, the population without electricity was dropped to 77 million or about 6% of China's total population. During the Ninth Five-Year Plan (1996–2000), the central government initiated the China Brightness Program to further extend the coverage of electricity services. The China Brightness Program focused on remote off-grid regions and promoted the adoption of wind and solar energy. After the power sector restructuring in 2002, the state grid corporations started to connect the isolated rural power grids and quickly expanded the service to cover almost the entire Chinese population. The population without electricity has dropped to less than 1% after 2010.

Reform and opening-up

In the late 1970s and early 1980s, the power supply was unstable, with frequent widespread outages. In order to relieve the shortage, the central government in 1981 decided to end the state monopoly and open up the power sector. Local governments, private enterprises, and even foreign investors were all allowed to build power plants in China. The opening-up policy effectively encouraged the investments in power generation, mostly in coal-fired power. A downside of this policy was that it led to the construction of numerous small coal-fired power plants. These small coal-fired power plants were inefficient and without proper emission control technology, and eventually became major contributors to air pollution.

In 1997, the State Power Corporation was established, and the Ministry of Electric Power Industry was abolished a year later. In 2002, the State Power Corporation was broken up into five state-owned power generation groups and two state grid corporations (Table 5.2).

The breakup was intended to encourage competition. This reorganization appeared to be effective, and the growth of power generation significantly picked up speed after 2002 (Figure 5.1).

Before 1993, China's power generation was consisted of only two types: hydropower and fossil fuel-fired power (predominantly coal). China's first nuclear power plant began commercial operation in 1993, and the share of nuclear power gradually increased to about 3% by 2015. The development of wind power started later than nuclear, but the growth has been faster than nuclear. Since 2012, wind power has become the third largest source of electricity in China. Solar photovoltaic electricity has been growing very fast since 2011, but still only accounted for 1% of electricity in 2015. This

Table 5.2 The separated power producer groups and grid corporations in 2002

Five major state-owned power groups	Two state grid corporations
Huaneng	State Grid Corporation of China (SGCC)
Huadian	China Southern Power Grid (CSG)
Guodian	
Datang	
China Power Investment (CPI)	

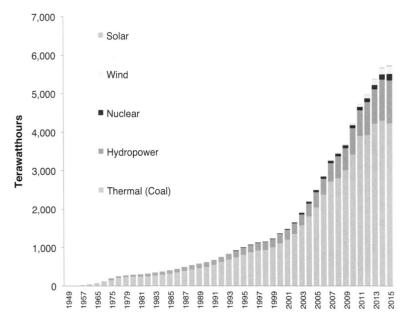

Figure 5.1 Annual national total power generation by sources
Source: BP (2016); CEC (2016)

chapter will focus mostly on coal-fired power. Hydro-, nuclear, wind, and solar power will be discussed in the following chapters.

The structure of the Chinese power industry is not as fragmented as the coal mining industry, but also not as concentrated as the oil and gas industry. Figure 5.2 shows the shares of electricity outputs of the top 10 producers in 2015. All the top 10 are state-owned. One of them (Sichuan Chuantou) is provincially supervised, while the other nine are supervised by the central government. The top five are the five major power groups (Huaneng, Huadian, Guodian, Datang, and China Power Investment/CPI) that originated from the 2002 breakup of the former State Power Corporation. Shenhua Guohau is a subsidiary of the state-owned coal mining company Shenhua. The Three Gorges Corporation specializes in hydropower. China General Nuclear (CGN) Power and the China National Nuclear Corporation (CNNC) are state-owned nuclear power companies. The rest (47%) of power generation was from a huge number of entities, including provincial state-owned companies, township and village enterprises, joint-ventures, and private companies.

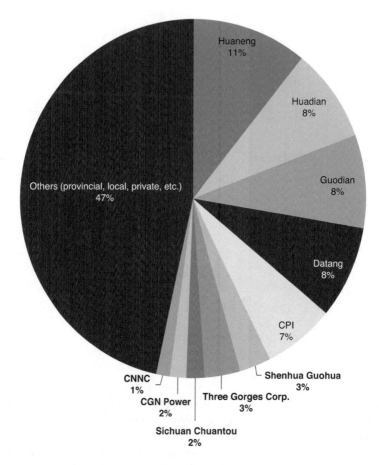

Figure 5.2 Shares of top 10 power generators in 2015
Source: BJX (2016)

Incomplete 2002 reform

The overarching goal of the power sector reform in 2002 was to break up monopoly and bring in market competition. The policymakers intended to establish a competitive wholesale electricity market in China. The policy agenda laid out several further steps after separating power generation from transmission. These next steps include separating supplementary assets from the core business, competitive bidding for selling power to the grid, and independent supervision.

In 2003, the State Electricity Regulatory Commission (SERC) was established as the supervisor of the foreseen electricity market. Unfortunately, the push for further reform encountered strong political resistances and all the pilot programs for competitive electricity sales failed. The NDRC continued to set electricity price administratively. Without electricity market, the SERC had nothing to supervise and became a research institute. In 2013, Chinese policymakers eventually acknowledged the failure and abolished SERC.

Due to the lack of transparency in China's policymaking, it is difficult to determine why the reform toward wholesale electricity market was suspended. Some pointed to the SGCC as the primary obstacle. A commentator pointed out the uncooperative attitude of the state grid corporations (Xiao, 2014), which have refused to reveal their transmission costs.

In 2011, an SERC official described the infighting between the NDRC and SERC, and indicated that the NDRC was unwilling to relinquish its pricing authority to the free market (People.com, 2011). As long as the NDRC controls the prices of electricity, it essentially controls the biggest determinant of power companies' profitability. Such power provided much room for corruption. In 2013, the vice chairman of NDRC and director of the National Energy Administration, Liu Tienan, was arrested for corruption charges and later sentenced to life in prison in 2014. The successor of Liu Tienan was Wu Xinxiong, former commissioner of the abolished SERC.

The unfortunate timing of the 2002 reform may also have contributed to its suspension. From 2002 to 2012, coal prices were volatile and rising quickly. Because the electricity prices were controlled, coal-fired power generators suffered financial losses. If the electricity prices were decontrolled during a power shortage, there is a high risk of runaway price hikes. Zhang Guobao, former vice chairman of NDRC and director of National Energy Administration (2008–2011), claimed that the suspension of 2002 reform was due to the concerns over power shortages (Xinhuanet, 2013).

Resumed reform in 2015

The growth rates of Chinese demand for electricity slowed down after 2010 (Figure 5.3). By 2015, overcapacity has become the primary challenge to energy policymakers. The overcapacity of electricity removed the fear of price hikes and created a new window of opportunity for power sector reform.

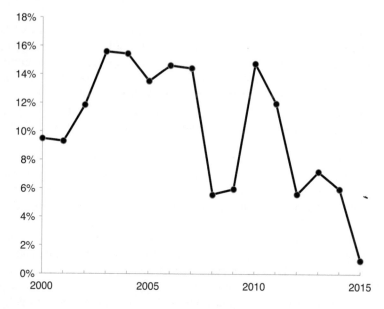

Figure 5.3 Annual growth rates of electricity consumption (2010–2015)
Source: NBS (2016)

In March 2015, the State Council announced a new round of electric power reform. The reform agenda, however, appeared to be more compromised than that in the 2002 reform. The 2015 reform no longer mentioned the competitive bidding mechanism for wholesale electricity sales, which is supposedly the key to establishing wholesale power market. Instead, the 2015 agenda highlighted the promotion of direct power purchase by large electricity users and the competition in retail markets.

Professor Wu Jiang of Renmin University has openly criticized the 2015 reform agenda as being severely compromised due to the influence of the State Grid Corporation of China (SGCC; Wu, 2015). He mentioned that, in the original draft, the reform aimed to establish independent power dispatch, which was revised as a "relatively independent" dispatch, because the SGCC was unwilling to relinquish its control over dispatch. By administratively dispatch power, the grid company decides which power producer gets to sell how much electricity. Without a competitive wholesale market, Chinese power producers cannot increase sales simply by lowering costs. In order to sell more electricity, Chinese power companies must maintain good relation with the state grid managers, perhaps with occasional gifts or bribes.

By 2016, more than 30 electricity trading centers were established to handle direct power purchases. All the trading centers are fully-owned or majority-owned subsidiaries of the state grid companies. It might be possible that the direct power purchases may eventually expanded into a de facto wholesale electricity market. By the time the book is written, the power sector reform is still an ongoing process. It is not yet clear whether China will eventually make its electricity sector competitive and market-driven.

Efficiency by scale and shutdown

China encouraged investments in small thermal (mostly coal-fired) power plants in the 1980s. Numerous small coal-fired power units were built. Over time, the low energy efficiencies and high air emissions of these small coal-fired plants became an increasing concern. In 1989, China started to impose restrictions on building new small coal-fired generators. In 1997, China started to order the shutdown of small thermal power generators. By the early 2000s, the shutdown of small thermal power has become a high-profile and high-priority energy policy (Xue et al., 2003).

The enforcement of the shutdown followed the target-responsibility system established in the national Five-Year Plans. The central government determined the national target for the total number of small coal-fired power plants to shut down each year, and the national target was broken down to each province. Each local government is responsible to meet its assigned target.

Most of the power plants in China are either state-owned or collectively owned, but some are privately owned. The mandated shutdown of power plants could in many cases be the forfeiture of private property. In the political culture of China, implementing environmental or industrial policies through forfeiture of properties appeared to be a commonly accepted practice.

In 1999, the State Council only ordered the shutdown of small thermal power plants that were no greater than 50 MW. Later on, the scope of shutdown was expanded to cover more power units. Additional criteria such as vintage, designed life, energy efficiency, and emission performance are added. Those that were more 20 years old and smaller than 100 MW were required to shut down. The plants that were smaller than 200 MW and have reached their original design life were also required to close down. Those with coal consumption per kWh of electricity 10% higher than the provincial average or 15% higher than the national average in 2005, and those failed to comply with emission standards, were also required to decommission.

In the 10th Five-Year Plan (2001–2005), the central government originally planned to shut down 14.2 GW of small thermal power, but only succeeded in shutting down 8.3 GW. The enforcement has been strengthened since then. The 11th Five-Year Plan (2006–2010) planned to shut down 50 GW small thermal plants and succeeded in closing down 73.8 GW.

A notable fact is that China continues to install new small coal-fired power units. The total coal-fired power capacity with unit scales smaller than 100 MW actually increased from 69.1 GW in 2000 to 108.1 GW in 2005 and 140.1 GW in 2010 (Xu et al., 2013).

During the 11th Five-Year Plan (2006–2010), the central government started to promote the policy called "shangda yaxiao," meaning "build the large, crush the small." The underlying philosophy is economy of scale. Large coal-fired power plants have many advantages over distributed small ones. A large boiler and steam generator may be designed to operate at higher pressure and higher temperature, and therefore has higher thermal efficiency than small ones. Equipping flue gas emission control devices at large thermal power plants is also more economical.

Every year, the China Electricity Council holds an energy efficiency contest for thermal power plants. All major power generators submit their energy performance records for competition. Although the power companies do not compete in sales due to the lack of electricity market, such contests provide alternative ways for the companies to compete against each other. The contests also provide useful data for performance benchmarks, which are used in evaluating power plants and their managers (Table 5.3). Despite the lack of electricity market, state-owned power producers do engage in non-market competitions. The performances of politically appointed managers are periodically reviewed based on a set of benchmarks. Those who perform well are more likely to be promoted, and those who miss too many benchmarks may be punished.

Over time, the national average thermal efficiency of coal-fired power plants benefited greatly from the "shangda yaxiao" policy. In the 1990s, the average thermal efficiencies of coal-fired power plants in China were much lower than those in the United States. China's efficiency surpassed the United States' in 2008 and kept rising, while the efficiencies of the U.S. coal-fired plants gradually declined as the plants aged (Figure 5.4).

The application of the "shangda yaxiao" approach is not limited to electric power. The Chinese government started to apply the "shangda yaxiao"

Table 5.3 Average performances of coal-fired power plants in China in 2011

Type	Water consumption (kg/kWh)	Thermal efficiency (%)
1 GW ultra supercritical once-through wet cooling	0.23	42.5%
1 GW ultra supercritical closed-loop wet cooling	2.11	42.2%
1 GW ultra supercritical dry cooling	0.23	38.9%
600 MW supercritical once-through wet cooling	0.26	40.2%
600 MW supercritical closed-loop wet cooling	1.95	40.2%
600 MW supercritical dry cooling	0.40	37.6%
600 MW subcritical once-through wet cooling	0.29	38.5%
600 MW subcritical closed-loop wet cooling	1.96	39.6%
600 MW subcritical dry cooling	0.29	36.8%
300 MW subcritical once-through wet cooling	0.37	37.1%
300 MW subcritical closed-loop wet cooling	2.31	37.1%
300 MW subcritical dry cooling	0.35	36.0%

Source: CEC (2012)

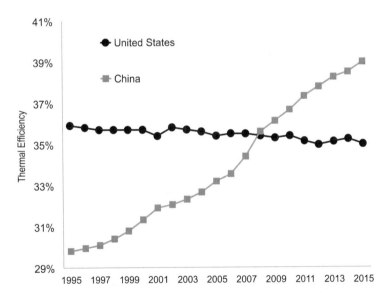

Figure 5.4 Average thermal efficiencies of coal-fired power plants in China and the United States

Source: Xu et al. (2013); CEC (2016); USEIA (2017)

principle in phasing out small and backward capacities in energy-intensive industries since the early 2000s. In 2005, the NDRC published the Industrial Structure Adjustment Guiding Catalog (NDRC, 2005), which classified industries into three types: encouraged, restricted, and to-be-retired. The Catalog was revised in 2011 and 2013. Based on the Guiding Catalog, the Chinese government actively implemented industrial policies to accelerate the capital turnovers in energy-intensive industries. Unlike the governments in Western market economies, the Chinese government does not avoid direct interventions in the market places and actively picks winners and losers in the industries on a routine basis.

Air-cooled coal-fired power

The widespread large-scale deployment of air-cooled coal-fired power plants is a rather unique development in China. Outside of China, coal-fired power plants are predominantly equipped with water-cooling towers.

The earliest Chinese attempt to develop air-cooling technologies for power plants occurred as early as the 1960s, but had no commercial success. In the late 1980s to early 1990s, a few air-cooled demonstration plants were built with imported components and licensed designs (Wang, 2006). However, these early systems encountered technical problems, and the market for air-cooled condensers remained very limited. The Chinese market for air-cooled power increased quickly after 2003, with the introduction of improved direct air-cooling technologies. In 2004, the NDRC mandated all coal-fired power plants in arid regions to use dry-cooling condensers. The political mandate essentially transformed the air-cooled coal-fired power from an exotic rarity to a mainstream technology.

By the early 2010s, about one-third of the new coal-fired power plants installed in China each year were air-cooled. The widespread use of air-cooling for coal-fired power is relatively unrecognized outside of China. Because the air-cooled condensers are more expensive and slightly less efficient (Table 5.3) than water-cooled ones, the applications are largely limited to the arid regions.

In the early years, two foreign suppliers dominated the market of air-cooling towers in China. In 2005, the State Council started to prioritize air-cooled thermal power plant in its targets for technology indigenization, and provided supports to Chinese air-cooling equipment producers. With favorable policies, Chinese equipment producers quickly expanded their market shares and took over more than half of the market after 2009 (Figure 5.5).

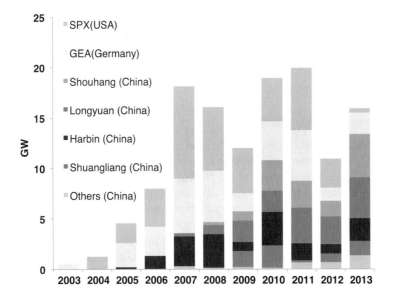

Figure 5.5 Market shares of major suppliers of air-cooled condensers for coal-fired power in China

Sources: Yang (2014), Zhang et al. (2014)

State grid empire

China's power grids were highly fragmented before the early 2000s. There were 11 major grids and thousands of small local grids all operating independently. The jurisdictions of the grids were also fragmented. The State Power Corporation was in charge of the major grids. The Ministry of Water Resources was responsible for the rural grids powered by small hydropower. The Ministry of Agriculture also managed many scattered grids in some regions.

The breakup of the State Power Corporation and founding of the two state grid corporations was a major divide in China's transmission development. The two state grid corporations enjoy tremendous monopoly powers. To the power producers, the grid company is the only buyer. Power generators' only alternative to the grid company's price and conditions were to shut down. To the power users, the state grid is the only supplier. The consumers' only alternative to the state grid is outage. The monopolistic powers provide the grid companies with great leverages in expansion and acquisitions.

The state grid corporations quickly integrated vast number of rural grids into their networks and consolidated the major grids into fewer and larger ones. Thanks to the double monopoly status, whatever the grid corporations spent was fully reimbursed by the electricity consumers. The seemingly unlimited budget led to the state grid corporation's aggressive expansion strategy.

Ultra-high-voltage transmission

In 2004, the SGCC proposed the idea of developing ultra-high-voltage (UHV) transmission technology and using it to strengthen the power grid. In 2005, with the approval of the NDRC, the SGCC started to design the demonstration projects of 1000 kV ultra-high-voltage alternating current (UHVAC) and 800 kV ultra-high-voltage direct current (UHVDC) transmissions.

The siting of the UHVAC demonstration project "Jindongnan – Nanyang – Jingmen" started in May 2006 and was done in three months. The construction began in August 2006 and was completed in 2009. Two UHVDC demonstration projects "Xiangjiaba – Shanghai" and "Yunnan – Guangdong" were also started in 2006 and completed in 2009 and 2010. Since then, China has built more than 12 UHV transmission projects, and many more are under construction and planned. China is currently the only country to widely utilize UHV transmission. High voltage enables the transmission lines to deliver a large amount of electricity over long distances with lower losses. For comparison, all the long-distance transmission lines in the United States are less than 500 kV.

Some experts have criticized the SGCC investments in UHV as not cost-effective. However, costs do not seem to be an important concern for SGCC. In addition to building the transmission lines, SGCC also acquired a manufacturer of transmission equipment so it can leverage its monopolistic power into equipment manufacturing. That acquisition was an open defiance to the 2002 reform agenda, which supposedly required grid corporations to focus on the core business of grid operation and separate non-core business.

In 2010, an article entitled "The State Grid Empire" in a Chinese business magazine described the story the SGCC acquisition and violation of the reform agenda (Wang, 2010). The magazine was soon suspended for a month for leaking internal information, which was not intended for the public (Zhai, 2010). In addition to silencing dissenting voices, the SGCC is also savvy in conducting propaganda campaigns in support of its goals. Since 2006, there have been plenty of news coverage, conferences, television programs, and books on the progress of the UHV development in China

(SGCC, 2017). UHV is widely celebrated as a showcase where China has leapfrogged into the technology leader of the world.

Merging four networks

In the 10th Five-Year Plan (2001–2005), the Chinese government proposed the idea of "merging three networks," which intended to combine the Internet, cable television, and telephone networks into one data-delivery network. In the 11th Five-Year Plan (2006–2010), the promotion of "merging three networks" was included again. In 2010, the SGCC proposed the idea of "merging four networks," to embed a data-delivering optical fiber in the power grid, and use the smart grid to also provide Internet, cable television, and telephone services. The SGCC conducted a few pilot projects to demonstrate the feasibility of "merging four networks." The telecommunication companies and cable television service providers, however, strongly opposed the idea. The State Council eventually rejected the proposal of "merging four networks." The SGCC continues to deploy the optical fiber composite low-voltage cables in its power grid, but claims it will only provide the infrastructure for telecommunication and cable television companies, but not to compete with them.

Electric cars

The SGCC has been actively involved in setting standards for electric vehicles in China. The SGCC offered to buy all the batteries and to rent them to electric car owners at subsidized prices. Instead of charging the batteries, electric car owners may simply swap their depleted batteries for fully charged ones (Jia, 2011). This business model will allow the SGCC to leverage its monopolistic power into the battery business. The SGCC proposal triggered a debate on whether China should build electric car charging stations or battery swapping stations. Unfortunately, Chinese car makers do not like to be controlled by the SGCC and opted for the charging model (21so. com, 2011).

Global energy interconnection

In 2015, Liu Zhenya, chairman of SGCC at the time, proposed the idea of global energy interconnection, and has been actively advertizing the idea. The SGCC established the Global Energy Interconnection Research Institute, Global Energy Interconnection Development and Cooperation Organization, and mobilized massive media campaigns, including an English book authored by Liu himself (Liu, 2015), to promote the idea.

The concept of global energy interconnection could justify the SGCC's aggressive overseas acquisition strategy. Since 2007, the SGCC has acquired transmission assets in the Philippines, Brazil, Portugal, Australia, Hong Kong, Italy, Belgium, Georgia, Ethiopia, and Pakistan, and more are under negotiation. Liu Zhenya was quoted saying, "In overseas acquisitions, money is not a problem for SGCC" (Yang, 2016). However, the dream of interconnecting these transmission lines into a global power grid still seems pretty remote.

Third-party online payment

In 2016, the SGCC launched its own third-party online payment platform. The SGCC platform offers a full range of third-party payment services, including online shopping, loan applications, wealth management, online travel booking, and many other services. Initially, news reports indicated that the SGCC planned to stop accepting electricity bill payments from the competing platforms, such as Alipay and WeChat Pay, so it could leverage its monopoly in electric power into eCommerce, and the banking and financial services (Ma, 2016). The anti-competitive intention was soon widely criticized, and the SGCC has announced that it will continue to accept electricity bill payments from other platforms (People's Daily, 2016).

Chapter highlights

- The structure of the Chinese power industry is not as fragmented as the coal mining industry, but also not as concentrated as the oil and gas industry.
- The power sector reform to establish electricity market started in 2002, but has remained incomplete.
- The Chinese government has effectively improved the efficiency of coal-fired power and energy-intensive industries by shutting down small plants and encouraging the construction of new big ones.
- Air-cooled coal-fired power has become a mainstream technology in China.
- The State Grid Corporation of China has been actively seeking to leverage its monopolistic powers in a wide range of businesses.

References

21so.com, 2011. *SGCC Battery Swap Model Not Welcome*. http://s.21so.com/search/index.php?r=qlinks/index&id=so_v9_21cbhnews_157049 (accessed 12/21/2016)

BJX, 2016. *Top 10 Power Companies 2015 Performance Ranking*. http://news.bjx.com.cn/html/20160504/729975.shtml (in Chinese) (accessed 12/20/2016)

BP, 2016. *Statistical Review of World Energy*. BP, London

CEC, 2012. *National Thermal Power Unit Benchmarking and Competition Dataset*. China Electricity Council, Beijing (in Chinese: 全国火电机组能效对标及竞赛资料, 中国电力企业联合会)

CEC, 2016. *2015 National Power Industry Statistical Table*. China Electricity Council, Beijing (in Chinese: 2015 全国电力工业统计数据一览表, 中国电力企业联合会)

Jia, H., 2011. *Electric Cars Will Start in 2011 Focus on Battery Swap Model*. http://auto.ifeng.com/news/special/xinnengyuanxize/20110111/509466.shtml (in Chinese) (accessed 12/21/2016)

Liu, Z., 2015. *Global Energy Interconnection*. Elsevier, Amsterdam

Ma, X., 2016. *SGCC Promote 95598pay; WeChat Pay and Alipay Will Not Be Able to Pay Electricity Bills*. http://tech.ifeng.com/a/20160503/41603009_0.shtml (in Chinese) (accessed 1/3/2017)

NBS, 2016. *China Energy Statistical Yearbook*. National Bureau of Statistics of China. http://data.stats.gov.cn/ (accessed 1/4/2017)

NDRC, 2005. *Industrial Structure Adjustment Guilding Catalog*. www.sdpc.gov.cn/fzgggz/fzgh/zcfg/200512/t20051222_65963.html (in Chinese) (accessed 12/21/2016)

People.com, 2011. *SERC Official Describes the Problem in Supervision; The Resistance to Power Reform Is Too Big*. http://energy.people.com.cn/GB/14971724.html (in Chinese) (accessed 12/20/2016)

People's Daily, 2016. *SGCC 95598pay: Market Competition Cannot Become Market Enclosure*. http://energy.people.com.cn/n1/2016/0704/c71661-28522442.html (in Chinese) (accessed 1/3/2017)

SGCC, 2017. *Ultra-High-Voltage Special Section*. www.sgcc.com.cn/ztzl/tgyzl/default.shtml (in Chinese) (accessed 12/22/2016)

USEIA, 2017. *Form EIA-923 Detailed Data*. U.S. Energy Information Administration. www.eia.gov/electricity/data/eia923/ (accessed 1/4/2017)

Wang, P.-Z., 2006. Air-cooled fossil-fired power units in China. *Fadian Shebei* 3, 174–177 (in Chinese: 王佩璋,我国空冷火电机组的实践,发电设备)

Wang, Q., 2010. State grid empire. *Business Watch Magazine* 220, March 5 (in Chinese: 王强,国网帝国,商务周刊)

Wang, Q., 2013. *2013 Energy Data*. Energy Foundation China, Beijing (in Chinese: 王庆一, 2013能源数据, 能源基金会)

Wu, J., 2015. *The Hidden Tricks in the No. 9 Document of Electricity Reform*. http://finance.sina.com.cn/zl/energy/20150330/112521842943.shtml (in Chinese) (accessed 12/21/2016)

Xiao, F., 2014. Transmission costs cannot be figured out in ten years, biggest obstacle to power reform. *China Business Journal*. http://finance.sina.com.cn/chanjing/cyxw/20140614/032819411122.shtml (in Chinese) (accessed 12/20/2016)

Xinhuanet, 2013. *The Abundance and Surplus of New Energy*. http://news.xinhuanet.com/politics/2013-05/05/c_115643883_3.htm (in Chinese) (accessed 12/20/2016)

Xu, Y., Yang, C.-J., Xuan, X., 2013. Engineering and optimization approaches to enhance the thermal efficiency of coal electricity generation in China. *Energy Policy* 60, 356–363

Xue, X., Li, J., Geng, Z., Zhu, X., Zheng, S., 2003. China's action of closing-down the small thermal power generation units. *Energy of China* 25(3), 9–12 (in Chinese: 薛新民, 李际, 耿志成, 朱兴珊, 郑爽, 中国的关停小火电行动, 中国能源)

Yang, C.-J., 2014. Brief history of air-cooled coal-fired power and its rapid adoption in China. *Cooling India*, May, 46–50

Yang, Q., 2008a. History of thermal power construction and development in China (1). *Electric Power Construction* 29(1), 98–101 (in Chinese: 杨勤明, 中国火电建设发展史(1), 电力建设)

Yang, Q., 2008b. History of thermal power construction and development in China (2). *Electric Power Construction* 29(2), 96–100 (in Chinese: 杨勤明, 中国火电建设发展史(2), 电力建设)

Yang, Y., 2016. *SGCC Ventures Overseas; Chairman Liu Zhenya: Money Not a Problem.* www.thepaper.cn/newsDetail_forward_1447199 (in Chinese) (accessed 12/22/2016)

Zhai, I., 2010. Magazine closed a month for criticizing power giant. *South China Morning Post*, May 10. www.scmp.com/article/713930/magazine-closed-month-criticising-power-giant (accessed 12/17/2016)

Zhang, C., Anadon, L.D., Mo, H., Zhao, Z., Liu, Z., 2014. Water-carbon trade-off in China's coal power industry. *Environmental Science & Technology* 48, 11082–11089

6 Hydropower

Hydropower has always been the second largest source of electricity in China. Unlike in developed countries, where the development of conventional large hydropower has nearly stopped and damming a large river is considered environmentally unsustainable, China is still building many new large hydropower projects by adding dams on rivers. The growth of hydropower capacity in China has indeed picked up speed since the early 2000s (Figure 6.1). Large-scale conventional hydropower is the dominant part of China's renewable energy.

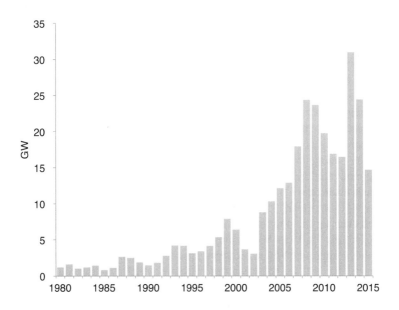

Figure 6.1 Annual addition of hydropower capacity

Source: CEC (2016)

The development of large hydropower plants has always been centrally planned and dominated by state-owned corporations. The largest players in China's hydropower industry include SinoHydro, China Three Gorges Corporation, China Gezhouba Group, and Sichuan Chuantou Energy Company. Small hydropower plants are mostly locally owned.

In 2015, China's installed hydropower capacity has reached 320 GW, and hydropower generation was 1126 terawatt-hours. For comparison, the United States has total installed hydropower capacity of 80 GW and output of 254 terawatt-hours in the same year. From 1949 to 2015, China's installed hydropower capacity increased by 1960 times, and its output has increased by 1567 times.

Hydropower in the planned economy

In the early years of the Communist China, the development of hydropower was much slower than coal-fired power. In the Soviet-supported 156 large industrial projects, only one hydropower project was included. Nevertheless, a few large hydropower projects, including Xinanjiang, Sanmenxia, Liujiaxia, Xinfengjiang, and Yilihe hydropower stations, started in the 1950s.

Among these earliest large hydropower projects, the Sanmenxia project was the most controversial (Tan and Liu, 2003). As soon as the project was proposed, the idea of building a dam on the mainstream of the Yellow River at Sanmenxia was immediately opposed by officials in the Shaanxi province and many hydrologists as well. The Yellow River got its name because it is muddy. Adding a dam on the Yellow River would inevitably cause the sediments to accumulate on the upstream, which is the Shaanxi province. The silt pileup would elevate the riverbed above the riversides and in the long term lead to frequent flooding.

Despite the controversies, the Communist leaders decided to proceed with the Sanmenxia project. Some indicated that the decision may be partially motivated by the decision-makers' eagerness to please Mao Zedong. There is an ancient Chinese saying/myth: "When a sage appears, the Yellow River will turn clear." By trapping the silts upstream, the Sanmenxia dam would clear up the downstream of Yellow River, and make Mao Zedong a sage. On July 18, 1955, Vice Premier Deng Zihui announced at the National People's Congress: "Within six years, after the completion of the Sanmenxia reservoir, we will see the clear Yellow River, which has been the people's dream for thousands of years."

The Sanmenxia project was completed in 1960. As expected, the upstream Guanzhong plain became frequently flooded and suffered tremendous damages. Over time, the Chinese government added several silt-releasing tunnels and pipes to remediate the damages, but could not completely reverse them. The Sanmenxia hydropower project is often considered one of the biggest failures in the Chinese history of water management.

During the construction of the Sanmenxia project, about 287,000 residents were relocated to make room for the reservoir. In 2010, a Chinese journalist Xie Chaoping published a book about the lives of the resettled population in the Sanmenxia project. He was soon arrested. The arrest of Xie triggered an outcry of protests from Chinese scholars, journalists, and writers. A month later, Xie was released on probation, but the book has been banned since then.

The unique ability to implement very large-scale involuntary resettlement has been one of China's strengths in infrastructure projects, and the construction of large hydropower projects has been the primary cause for resettlement. Under the planned economy, the government controls lands, housing, education, employment, and the rationing of food and many other necessities. Such controls made it very difficult for people to refuse involuntary resettlement. The World Bank estimated that the Chinese government resettled 4.6 million people in the 1950s for water reservoir projects, 3.2 million in the 1960s, 1.4 million in the 1970s, and 1 million in the 1980s (Travers, 1993).

Most of the dams built in the 1950s were for irrigation instead of hydropower. During the Great Leap Forward, tens of thousands of small dams were built, but most of them were poorly constructed and unfit for hydropower (Kang, 2013). Rural electrification was not a priority during this period.

In the 1950s, the First Ministry of Machine-Building organized the technology transfer of the hydraulic generator from the Soviet Union and started to manufacture indigenous generators at Harbin Electric Machinery Factory. Since then, the central government has continued to organize technology transfer, research and development (R&D), and indigenization of equipment manufacturing. Over time, China gradually developed indigenous capacities in the entire supply chain of hydropower, including geological survey, R&D, design, construction, equipment manufacturing, operation and maintenance.

After the Sino-Soviet split in 1960, Mao initiated the "Third Front" strategy, which was to move military industries to inland provinces and to prepare for potential invasions by both the Soviet Union and the United States. As a result, the focus of hydropower development shifted to the middle and upper reaches of Yangtze River. At first, the Three Gorges site was proposed. Mao Zedong decided that the cost of the Three Gorges would overburden the national budget.

A smaller project, Gezhouba, was chosen instead. The purpose of the Gezhouba hydropower plant was to provide electricity to the inland military industries. Because Mao believed the war to be imminent, he wanted to develop Gezhouba with great urgency. The construction started in 1970 before the geological survey and dam design were done. The parallel implementation of geological survey, dam design, and construction caused a great deal of confusions and conflicts. In 1972, the construction was suspended for two years to conduct supplemental surveys and to revise designs. The original estimate of five-year construction was eventually proven to be overly optimistic. The construction of Gezhouba hydropower project eventually took 18 years, and was completed in 1988.

Hydropower after 1978 reform

After Mao's death, the new leader Deng Xiaoping focused his attention on economic development. The People's Republic of China established diplomatic relations with the United States in 1979. China opened itself up to investments from the western capitalist world. The Lubuge dam was the first Chinese hydropower project built with loans from the World Bank.

Lubuge

The World Bank loan for Lubuge project was approved in 1984. To help China open up to foreign contractors, the World Bank required international competitive bidding (ICB) for the headrace tunnel at Lubuge. The headrace tunnel was chosen as the first test case of ICB demonstration in China, because the construction process is highly mechanized. The low demand on local manpower made it easier for a foreign contractor to manage. Grants from Australian, Norwegian, and Canadian governments also helped convince the Chinese to use Western engineering consultants for the first time in the history of the People's Republic (World Bank, 1993).

The Japanese Taisei Corporation won the bidding for the headrace tunnel. In addition to sending its own management team, the Taisei Corporation also employed workers from the China Hydropower No. 14 Engineering Bureau. The construction proceeded much more quickly and efficiently than other similar projects in China. Chinese workers were very impressed by the advanced machinery and construction management system, and started to introduce new ideas in the No. 14 Bureau. This started the modernization of hydropower and civil construction in China. Chinese civil engineers refer to the experiences as the "Lubuge Shock Waves," which have profound impacts on modernizing the practices in construction finance, procurement, and project management (Zhang, 2014).

Ertan

The Ertan hydropower project was the first Chinese hydropower project to be entirely contracted through international competitive bidding following the FIDIC rules. FIDIC is the French abbreviation for the International Federation of Consulting Engineers, an international standard organization. This project provided Chinese construction firms the opportunities to familiarize themselves with international contracting practices, and therefore prepared them for the competitive environment under the World Trade Organization (WTO), which China joined in 2001. With international consulting services and training, the project also helped introduce modern construction technologies. The Ertan project started in 1991 and was completed in 1999, becoming the largest hydropower plant in China at that time. From a technical perspective, this project was generally deemed very successful.

Soon after the Ertan hydropower station started to operate, it quickly accumulated huge financial losses. Due to local protectionism, the Sichuan provincial power company would only buy less than half of the output from the Ertan station. Instead, the Sichuan power company purchased a large amount of power from small coal-fired stations, which were far more expensive and dirtier. The Sichuan power company explained that they did so to keep the 2000 jobs in the local economy (CCTV, 2002). The financial mess was eventually resolved in 2002 by building a new transmission line to deliver the power from Ertan to Shanghai, which is more than 2000 kilometers away.

China greatly improved its hydropower technology and construction capability during the 1990s, and started to build very large hydropower plants. Ertan station quickly dropped from being China's largest hydropower station in 1999 to the 10th largest in 2015. Among these very large hydropower stations, the Three Gorges project is the largest and also the most controversial.

Three gorges

Dr. Sun Yat-sen was the first to propose the idea of the Three Gorges dam in 1919. The Nationalist government did some preliminary works in 1932, and invited the U.S. Bureau of Reclamation chief design engineer, John L. Savage, to assist with the project in 1944. In an attempt to seek financial support from U.S. President Franklin Roosevelt for the Three Gorges project, Generalissimo Chiang Kai-shek offered to name it Roosevelt Dam. The Nationalist government never got the chance to build the dam before it was defeated by the Communists.

In 1955, the Chinese government invited experts from the Soviet Union to assist in the survey of potential dam sites throughout the Yangtze River, including the Three Gorges. In 1956, Chinese officials had started to debate on whether China should start with this project as soon as possible or build smaller projects first and postpone the Three Gorges for later. There were also debates on whether the proposed Three Gorges dam should be primarily designed for flood control or be a multiple-purpose project with hydropower and navigation functions. The debates soon escalated into political infightings between the Yangtze Valley Planning Office (YVPO) and the Ministry of Electric Power. The most prominent leaders of the two sides were Lin Yishan, head of YVPO, and Li Rui, former Vice Minister of Electric Power. In 1959, Li Rui was labeled as anti-party and sent to prison when Mao Zedong launched the "anti-rightist campaign" against those who criticized his mistakes in the Great Leap Forward (Lieberthal and Oksenberg, 1988).

In the 1960s, Mao decided to postpone the Three Gorges project so he could focus his attention on preparing for World War III. After Mao's death, Li Rui was released after 20 years in prison and became a Vice Minister of Water Resources and Electric Power in 1979.

The debates over the Three Gorges continued for more than another decade. Finally, in 1992, the National People's Congress approved the Three Gorges project: 1767 representatives voted in favor, 177 voted against, and 664 abstained. The National People's Congress was typically a rubber stamp that approved everything unanimously. The Three Gorges project was an extremely rare case where so many representatives dared to abstain or even vote against it (Wang, 2013).

The construction started in 1994. More than 1.2 million people were resettled. The hydropower generation began in 2003. Since its completion, the Three Gorges hydropower has been the largest hydropower station in the world.

China's hydropower resource survey in 2003 identified 694 GW of theoretical potential hydropower resources, 542 GW of technically available hydropower resources, and 402 GW of economically feasible hydropower capacities (Zhang, 2010). In 2007, the NDRC published the Renewable Energy Mid- to Long-Term Plan, which projected that China's installed hydropower capacity will reach 300 GW by 2020. Since then, the growth has exceeded that target. The 13th Five-Year Plan (2016–2020) of Hydropower expects the installed hydropower capacity to reach 380 GW by 2020.

Small hydropower

The Chinese government defines small hydropower as hydropower units of less than 50 MW rating, which is probably the largest of all definitions of small hydro in the world. Although there is no international consensus on the precise definition of small, a value of up to 10 MW is more common (Small-hydro.com, 2016).

Unlike in most developed countries, where small hydropower is generally considered more environmentally benign than large-scale hydropower, the reputation of small hydropower in China is rather tainted. Small hydropower stations are often considered unsafe and environmentally harmful.

In the 1980s and 1990s, the widespread deployment of small hydropower stations had played a pivotal role in China's rural electrification. After the success of rural electrification, the Ministry of Water Resources abolished its division on hydropower and rural electrification in 1998, and many local governments also rescinded their corresponding departments. The reorganization created a regulatory vacuum. The installations of small hydro continued in anarchy. Numerous small hydro stations were built with no (documented) plan, no review (on environmental impacts, safety, etc.), no supervision, and no inspection, which were later referred to as "4-No." Many small hydro incidents, including dam failures, soil erosion, deforestation, and illegal construction in nature reserves were reported in the news (Xinhuanet, 2006; 2011). Some small hydropower stations even drained the river flows and rendered the downstream completely waterless (China.com, 2010).

In 2003, the Ministry of Water Resources started to investigate the "4-No" small hydro stations. In 2006, the Ministry issued a notice to stop the "disorderly development" of small hydro and shut down "4-No" stations. Despite the efforts, small hydro incidents continued to occur. It is not yet clear whether China will figure out an effective way to resolve the problems.

By 2015, China has built more than 47,000 small (<50MW) hydropower stations with a combined capacity of 75 GW. The 13th Five-Year Plan (2016–2020) of Hydropower expects China's total installation of small hydropower to reach 80 GW by 2020.

Pumped hydroelectric energy storage

China is a latecomer in utilizing pumped hydroelectric stations for energy storage, but it is catching up very quickly (Figure 6.2). The earliest pumped hydro station in China was a very small one built in 1968. The development remained slow until a major policy change in 2004.

Before 2004, most of the pumped hydro facilities in China were built by local governments and local power companies. The pricing scheme varied from case to case. The uncertain business model deterred investment. In 2004, the NDRC decided that pumped hydro stations are transmission facilities and should be constructed and managed by the grid companies,

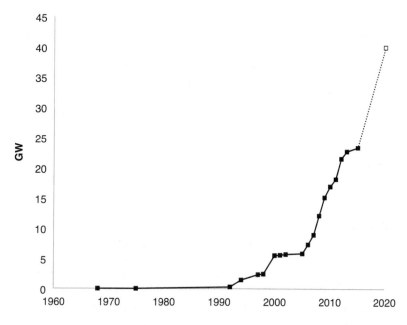

Figure 6.2 Installed pumped hydro capacities and projection for 2020
Source: NEA (2016); Yang (2016)

and stipulated that the construction and operation costs of pumped hydro stations should be incorporated into the operation costs of the state grid companies (Yang, 2016). As explained in Chapter 5, the state grid corporations are rich and powerful organizations with very aggressive expansion strategies. The decision to designate pumped hydro stations as transmission facilities immediately jump-started the rapid buildup of pumped hydro. China's installed pumped hydro energy storage capacity more than quadrupled from 2004 to 2015. The 13th Five-Year Plan of Hydropower prioritizes the development of pumped hydro energy storage and expects the installed capacity to reach 40 GW by 2020. The National Energy Administration also predicts that China's pumped hydro capacity may reach 90 GW by 2025.

There are at least two reasons to expect the very aggressive buildup of pumped hydro to continue. First, China is increasing its renewable energy to mitigate global warming and air pollution. The intermittent nature of wind and solar energy is driving the demand for more energy storage on the power grid. Pumped hydroelectric energy storage is the lowest-cost and most mature grid-scale energy storage technology. The buildup of pumped hydro energy storage will help accommodate more renewable energy into the power grids. Second, the growth of the Chinese economy has slowed down significantly since 2014. With overcapacities in most industries, the Chinese government is eagerly looking for new targets to invest in. Pumped hydro is a rare area where there is no overcapacity. With ample demand and favorable policies, China's pumped hydro capacity will likely be skyrocketing in the coming decade.

Overseas hydropower contracting

Before 2000, China was largely absent in international hydropower contracting business, except for some very small projects. However, with gradually accumulated domestic construction experiences, Chinese hydropower construction firms have become increasingly competitive after 2000. The leading companies include SinoHydro, China Gezhouba Group Company, and China International Water & Electric Corp. These companies are increasingly active in international hydropower contracting, and sometimes even compete in non-hydropower infrastructure projects. In 2015, the combined revenues of overseas projects of these three companies have reached US$15 billion (MOC, 2016).

Chapter highlights

- The construction of conventional large hydropower in China has accelerated since the early 2000s.
- Large hydropower plants that dam rivers constitute the dominant share of China's renewable energy.
- China is uniquely capable of implementing very large-scale involuntary resettlement for the construction of large hydropower projects.
- Small hydropower has a tainted reputation in China.
- China is quickly building a large number of pumped hydroelectric energy storage stations.
- Chinese state-owned construction companies have become active players in international contracting business.

References

CCTV, 2002. *Ertan Power Station: My Spring Is Coming.* www.cctv.com/financial/jingji/sanji/jujiao/20020426/125.html (in Chinese) (accessed 12/23/2016)

CEC, 2016. *2015 National Power Industry Statistical Table.* China Electricity Council, Beijing (in Chinese: 2015 全国电力工业统计数据一览表, 中国电力企业联合会)

China.com, 2010. *4-no Stations Trap Water Predatorily.* www.china.com.cn/
    economic/txt/2010-02/25/content_19472260.htm (in Chinese) (12/24/2016)
Kang, X., 2013. *Hydropower Development in China: History and Narratives.*
    Improving Hydropower Decision-making Processes in the Mekong Basin Project.
    https://wle-mekong.cgiar.org/projects/mk8/ (accessed 12/22/2016)
Lieberthal, K., Oksenberg, M., 1988. *Policy Making in China: Leaders, Structures,
    and Processes.* Princeton University Press, Princeton, NJ
MOC, 2016. *2015 Top 100 Companies in China's Overseas Contracting.* Ministry of
    Commerce. www.mofcom.gov.cn/article/tongjiziliao/dgzz/201602/20160201250935.
    shtml (in Chinese) (accessed 12/24/2016)
NEA, 2016. *Thirteenth Five-Year Plan for Hydropower Development.* National Energy
    Administration, Beijing (in Chinese: 国家能源局, 水电发展"十三五"规划)
Small-hydro.com, 2016. *Small Scale Hydropower.* www.small-hydro.com/about/
    small-scale-hydrpower.aspx (accessed 12/24/2016)
Tan, Y., Liu, H., 2003. *Sanmenxia Dam: Once the First in China, Now Dying.*
    www.people.com.cn/GB/huanbao/1072/2206736.html (in Chinese) (accessed
    12/22/2016)
Travers, L., 1993. *China Involuntary Resettlement.* World Bank. Report No. 11641-
    CHA
Wang, S., 2013. *Media Comments on the Changes in Voting: Opposing Votes Reflect the
    Progress in Democracy.* http://news.163.com/13/0316/02/8Q29VKIA00014AED.
    html (in Chinese) (accessed 12/23/2016)
World Bank, 1993. *Project Completion Report.* China Lubuge Hydroelectric Project
    (Loan 2382-CHA)
Xinhuanet, 2006. *Ministry of Water Resources Stop Disorderly Development;
    Remove '4-no' Stations.* http://news.xinhuanet.com/politics/2006-08/29/content_
    5021345.htm (in Chinese) (accessed 12/24/2016)
Xinhuanet, 2011. *Many Small Hydro Stations Built Without License in Zhouqu,
    Gansu; Government: We Cannot Control Them.* http://news.xinhuanet.com/
    local/2011-08/03/c_121761842.htm (in Chinese) (accessed 12/24/2016)
Yang, C.-J., 2016. Pumped hydroelectric storage. pp. 25–38. In Letcher, T.M. ed.
    Storing Energy: With Special Reference to Renewable Energy Sources. Amster-
    dam: Elsevier
Zhang, G., 2010. *100 Years of Hydropower in China.* http://energy.people.com.cn/
    GB/12548272.html (in Chinese) (accessed 12/23/2016)
Zhang, J., 2014. *A Century of Hydropower Development in China.* www.ctgpc.com.
    cn/sxjt/sdbl/_303760/585234/index.html (in Chinese) (accessed 12/23/2016)

7   Nuclear power

The nuclear power industry in China is completely dominated by the state. However, the national policymakers encountered a great deal of difficulties in enforcing national policies. The state-owned nuclear corporations have in many cases resisted national policies for their corporate interests. China is leading the global nuclear renaissance by building more nuclear power plants than anywhere else. Whether China will really need that much electricity is however increasingly questioned after the 2014 economic slowdown.

Early years

China started building a nuclear industry in the late 1950s, but its nuclear industry was exclusively for military purposes until the 1980s. In 1981, the Ministry of Nuclear Industry decided to start developing an indigenously designed nuclear power station. The Qinshan site was chosen in 1982, and construction started in 1983. In 1988, the Ministry of Nuclear Industry was reorganized as the China National Nuclear Corporation (CNNC), which continued to build the Qinshan Station. The Qinshan Phase 1 was completed at the end of 1991. The commercial operation started in 1994 after two years of testing.

Meanwhile, in 1979, the Guangdong provincial government and the Ministry of Water Resources and Electric Power started to develop a nuclear power project in Guangdong province to sell electricity to Hong Kong, which was still a British colony at that time. The State Council approved the Daya Bay project in 1982. The Guangdong Nuclear Power Investment Company was soon established, and with a Hong Kong-based power company formed a joint venture to build, own, and operate the Daya Bay project. In 1987, the joint venture chose the French company Framatome as contractor and equipment supplier. The Unit 1 of Daya Bay Station started operation in 1993 and Unit 2 in 1994. With the successful completion of the Daya

Table 7.1 Nuclear power projects in the Ninth Five-Year Plan

Project name	Reactor type	Source of technology	Owner	Completion
Qinshan Phase 2	CNP-600	Indigenous	CNNC	2002, 2004
Qinshan Phase 3	PHWR-CANDU	Canada	CNNC	2002, 2003
Tianwan Phase 1	VVER-1000	Russia	CNNC	1999, 2000
Ling Ao Phase 1	PWR	France	CGN	2002, 2003

Bay project, the State Council decided to establish the China Guangdong Nuclear Power Group (CGN)[1] to build more plants.

In the burgeoning stage, the Chinese civilian nuclear industry followed two parallel paths, which later caused a great deal of political infightings and difficulties in standardization.

Four nuclear power projects started during the Ninth Five-Year Plan (1996–2000). The CNNC has three and the CGN has one (Table 7.1). At this time, China widely tried out various designs of nuclear reactors. Each of the four projects adopted a different design. These reactors with diverse designs were completed during 1999 to 2004.

As a latecomer in civilian nuclear power, Chinese policymakers were eager to learn from the experiences in the developed countries. From a technical perspective, trying out many designs may have been a good way to allow Chinese nuclear engineers to learn from the various technical features of different nuclear reactors. From a managerial perspective, however, many studies have pointed out that standardization was the key that made the French nuclear power program relatively more successful than the American one. China's diverse choices of designs in the 1990s were contrary to the French approach.

Endless fights for standardization

By the early 2000s, many Chinese technocrats were calling for standardization. In 2003, the State Council decided to adopt advanced technology and develop a unified national technology roadmap. After a series of debates and expert consultations, the NDRC eventually chose AP1000 as the preferred standard. At that time, all the nuclear generators in China followed designs that were categorized as Generation II designs. The AP1000 design is a Generation III design, which has higher safety standard than Generation II, at least in theory.

CGN and CNNC, however, continued to criticize this choice, and argued that AP1000 lacks a proven construction record and that it is risky to deploy an untried design. The CGN preferred to keep using its own improved Generation II CPR1000 design, which has accumulated experiences in construction and operation. The CNNC also preferred to keep developing its own design. Unable to convince the two state-owned corporations to follow national policy, the Chinese government established the State Nuclear Power Technology Corporation (SNPTC) to handle the technology transfer and indigenization of AP1000.

Yu Zusheng, former deputy director of Nuclear Safety Center, has described the political infightings between the NDRC and CNNC/CGN with the analogy of rebellious sons: "Neither of your sons would listen to you. Their conflicts of interests cannot be resolved. Therefore you have to give birth to a third son to carry out national policy" (Ma et al. 2011).

The policy debates postponed the development of nuclear power during the 10th Five-Year Plan (2001–2005). Only one nuclear power project (Ling Ao Phase 2) started construction in this period. During this time, the demand for electricity grew much faster than expected, and power shortages became an increasing concern.

During the early 2000s, there was a debate over "one-step" or "two-step" strategy (Wen, 2007). The SNPTC preferred the "one-step" strategy, which was to stop approving new nuclear power projects to wait until the completion of AP1000 demonstrations. The CNNC and CGN advocated the "two-step" strategy, which was to keep building their Generation II reactors in the near term to relieve power shortage, and switch to Generation III designs later.

Due to the concern for power shortages, the NDRC accepted the two-step strategy and started to approve many nuclear power projects. By 2005, the official slogan for nuclear power policy, "moderate development," has been replaced by "speed up and push forward" (CEC, 2005). In 2007, the NDRC set the 2020 target of nuclear power capacity as 40 GW (NDRC, 2007). By 2010, the target has been revised upward to 70–80 GW (MOST, 2010). During the 11th Five-Year Plan (2006–2010), the State Council approved 13 nuclear power projects with a total of 34 reactors and combined capacity of 37 GW (NEA, 2012).

Fukushima disaster

By March 11, 2011, when the Fukushima Daiichi nuclear disaster happened, 28 nuclear reactors were under construction. The designs of these reactors were rather diverse (Table 7.2).

The Fukushima Daiichi nuclear disaster was a big shock to the whole world. Five days after the nuclear disaster, an article by Wang Binghua, chairman of the State Nuclear Power Technology Corporation (SNPTC),

Table 7.2 Nuclear reactors under construction
in China on March 11, 2011

Design	Number of reactors
AP1000	4
CNP1000	5
CNP600	3
CPR1000	14
EPR1750	2

appeared on the *Qiushi* magazine, which is a Communist Party publication widely circulated among high-level policymakers (Wang, 2011). The entire content of this article was soon reprinted in several newspapers. In this article, Wang argued that new nuclear power projects should adopt the safest design, and that China should focus its efforts on the AP1000 reactor.

Before the Fukushima event, CNNC and CGN had always advocated against the SNPTC over the choice of AP1000, and argued that their improved versions of Generation II reactors were already safe enough. However, after Fukushima, CNNC and CGN did not argue against Wang's opinion, or at least not openly.

After the Fukushima incident, the State Council suspended the approval of new nuclear projects, and ordered a comprehensive safety inspection of all existing nuclear facilities. The inspection reported no finding of any serious safety issue (MEP/NEA/CEA, 2012). In 2012, the State Council approved the report on "Nuclear Safety and Radioactive Pollution Control 12th Five-Year Plan and 2020 Long-Term Target," which specified that all future nuclear power projects must adopt "more mature and advanced reactor types" and "reasonably control the speed and scale of deployment before the technology of most advanced safety standards has been fully tested." Although the wordings were a bit ambiguous, in essence, they meant that all new projects must adopt Generation III designs, and the speed of nuclear power buildup will be scaled back to wait for the testing of Generation III designs. The previous "two-step" strategy was replaced by "one-step." The official slogan of "speed up and push forward" was reverted back to "moderate development," and the 2020 target was scaled down to 58 GW. The approval of new nuclear power projects resumed at the end of 2012. Many new projects have been approved since then.

Except for those that were already under construction, all new projects previously proposed with Generation II designs were required to change their designs to Generation III. However, this new policy did not exactly require all the new projects to adopt AP1000 design, and allowed CNNC and CGN to keep resisting AP1000 by developing their own Generation III reactors.

Hualong 1

In order to compete with AP1000, the CNNC developed its Generation III design ACP1000, and CGN came up with ACPR1000+. In 2013, the National Energy Administration asked the CNNC and CGN to standardize their two designs into one, and reportedly has threatened that if they refuse, projects of ACP1000 or ACPR1000+ will never be approved for construction. With increased pressure to standardize, the CNNC and CGN agreed to unify their designs.

In 2014, the CNNC and CGN each announced their Hualong 1 design separately, on different days and at different press conferences. Sun Qin, chairman of CNNC, has acknowledged that the CNNC version of Hualong 1 is not exactly the same as the CGN version of Hualong 1, but insisted that the differences are minor. Others, however, have suggested that the differences may be more than minor (Energy, 2014; Lin, 2016).

Meanwhile, the SNPTC also developed the CAP1400, which is the indigenized version of AP1000. The Chinese government claimed that AP1000 and CAP1400 were still the officially preferred choices for nuclear power stations in China, and the development of Hualong 1 was intended primarily for overseas projects. The CNNC and CGN have argued that the overseas sales of Hualong 1 reactors would be impossible without prior domestic construction and operation records. Therefore, a domestic demonstration project of the CNNC version of Hualong 1 reactors has been approved and started construction at the Fuqing stations, and another demonstration of the CGN version of Hualong 1 has also started at the Fangchenggang station.

In the 13th Five-Year Plan of Electric Power Development, the 2020 target for nuclear power capacity has remained 58 GW (Figure 7.1). The nuclear power construction business in China has become by far the largest in the world (Figure 7.2). China's economic growth, however, has slowed down significantly since 2014, and the electric power industry has been burdened with huge overcapacity. Whether China still needs as many new nuclear power plants as previously planned is rather questionable.

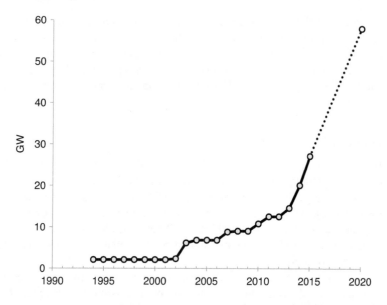

Figure 7.1 Installed nuclear power capacities and projection for 2020
Source: CEC (2016)

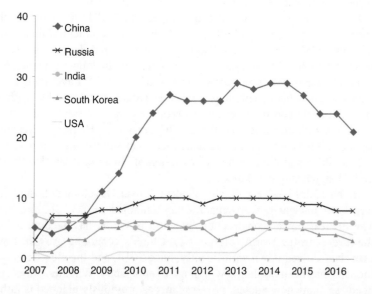

Figure 7.2 Number of nuclear reactors under construction
Source: WNA (2016a)

Pricing

The price of nuclear electricity is administratively set based on a cost-plus principle. Before 2013, after each nuclear power plant was completed, the NDRC determined the electricity price for this particular power plant based on its costs plus a certain amount of profit. The cost-plus pricing method guaranteed that a nuclear power project would always be profitable regardless of its cost.

In 2013, the NDRC revised its pricing practice for nuclear power by setting a unified benchmark price for all new nuclear power plant (Zhu, 2013). The nuclear power benchmark price was set at 0.43 RMB per KWh, which was higher than the prices of all existing nuclear power plants. Therefore, the benchmark price is high enough to make almost all nuclear power projects profitable. Some of the demonstrations, such as the AP1000 and Hualong 1 projects, will likely have higher costs. They may be exempted from the benchmark pricing system and still follow the cost-plus pricing approach.

The benchmark pricing scheme in China is the same as the feed-in tariffs in other countries. The difference is that, in other countries, the feed-in tariff system is meant to accelerate the adoption of renewable energy. In China, benchmark pricing was first applied to coal-fired power in 2004, and extended to onshore wind power in 2009, photovoltaic electricity in 2011, and nuclear power in 2013 (IESM, 2014).

The pricing scheme made nuclear power a very good business. Several major coal-fired power producers are also interested in entering the nuclear business. The Chinese government has limited the nuclear licenses to the three national nuclear companies: CNNC, CGN, and SNPTC.

Merger of SNPTC and CPI

Despite being the carrier of the officially preferred AP1000 design, the SNPTC was disadvantaged in its competition against the CNNC and CGN. Both the CNNC and CGN enjoy the doubled status as both reactor vendor and power generator. They may develop their own reactors, build them, and then sell electricity for profits. SNPTC, however, has been strictly a reactor vendor and technology provider. SNPTC was supposed to sell its AP1000 reactors to CNNC and CGN. Selling to your competitors is never easy. Therefore, despite being the favorite son, SNPTC was also the weakest in the Chinese nuclear oligarchy.

In 2015, the Chinese central government decided to merge the SNPTC with the China Power Investment (CPI) Corporation, which was one of the five major state-owned power generators. The newly created State Power

Investment Corporation (still using the CPI logo and brand) will have both nuclear reactor and power generation businesses. The merger more than leveled the playing field for the SNPTC, because CPI has a much larger market share in electric power than CGN and CNNC (Figure 5.2 in Chapter 5). In 2015, the CPI contributed 7% of electric power in China, while CGN produced 2% and CNNC 1%.

Technology indigenization

Since the beginning of China's nuclear power development, technology transfer and indigenization have always been important parts of the nuclear energy policy. As early as 1983, the State Council had listed large nuclear power equipment in its national target for indigenization. The Chinese government set targets for domestic content ratios for each nuclear power project and reviewed their performance on a routine basis.

The Chinese government is never shy in picking winners. The Nuclear Power Medium and Long-Term Development Plan (2005–2020) explicitly pointed out that nuclear equipment manufacturing will mainly rely on the tree companies: Dongfang Electric Manufacturing Company, Shanghai Electric Company, and Harbin Electric Corporation (NEA, 2011). The plan also stipulated that, for the components that China already can make, their procurements will be exclusively from domestic suppliers. For those China cannot make, China adopted a strategy of "market for technology," which was to offer a small piece of the market to foreign suppliers in exchange for technology transfers.

Nuclear-grade heavy forging is another focus of indigenization, where the two chosen ones are China First Heavy Industries and China National Erzhong Group (meaning "China Second Heavy Industries" in Chinese). With focused government supports and nearly exclusive access to Chinese market, the Chinese government has successfully made its selected winners the leading nuclear component suppliers.

High-temperature pebble-bed reactor

Tsinghua University started to develop a high-temperature air-cooled pebble-bed reactor in the 1980s. The 10-MW test module HTR-10 was completed in 2000 and reached full capacity in 2003. In 2005, China decided to scale up the HTR design for commercial applications. A joint venture of Huaneng Group, CNNC, and Tsinghua University was established in 2007 to finance the 200-MW HTR-200 demonstration at the Shidaowan Nuclear Power Station. The construction began in 2012 and the completion is expected in 2017. This project will be the first commercial demonstration of any Generation IV nuclear power reactor in the world. With its development of Generation IV reactors, Chinese policymakers are hoping to leapfrog ahead and become the technology leader in nuclear power in the world.

Site selection

Unlike most other countries, the siting of nuclear power station in China is relatively easy. China only allows two types of land ownerships: state-owned and collectively owned. All urban lands are state-owned, and most rural lands are collectively owned. There is no private land in China. The central government has the right to convert any collectively owned lands to state-owned. The unique land ownership system greatly alleviates the "not in my backyard" (NIMBY) problem. If local residents do not like having a nuclear power station in their backyard, they have few choices other than to give up their homes and move away. Legally speaking, the state owns everyone's backyard.

Nevertheless, disputes over the sites of proposed nuclear power stations have occurred in some cases. The siting of the Pengze project in Jiangxi province is probably the most famous case. The Pengze site is located adjacent to the provincial border between Jiangxi and Anhui. The Wangjiang county of Anhui province sits right across the Yangtze River from the Pengze nuclear power site. Normally, the local government is responsible for silencing local protesters. In this particular case, neither the Pengze county government nor the Jiangxi provincial government has jurisdiction over the neighboring Wangjiang county. A few retired government officials in Wangjiang initiated the petition to stop the Pengze nuclear power project. The Wangjiang county magistrate supported the protest and issued a formal appeal against the Pengze project in 2011. The appeal indicated that the Pengze project falsified the population data and manipulated public opinion surveys. Furthermore, the Pengze project claimed to have acquired a water resource certificate from the Yangtze River Basin Water Resources Protection Bureau, but the bureau denied ever receiving any application from the Pengze project. Despite the disputes and accusations, the National Nuclear Safety Administration has reconfirmed in 2012 that the siting of Pengze project has satisfied all regulations (Jiang, 2011; Hook, 2012).

There have also been some sporadic protests over other nuclear sites. For example, local residents near the Hongshiding nuclear power site organized a petition against the project via the Internet in 2007. The local government arranged informal meetings with the petitioners to listen to their opinions. However, in the official environmental assessment review, only one opponent was allowed to attend so he was outvoted by 19 to 1 (He, 2008). So far, no local opposition has ever been able to stop or delay any nuclear power project in China.

Radioactive waste depository

The Chinese government seems to have little difficulty in siting and building radioactive waste depositories, likely thanks to its unique ability in silencing local opposition. Most of the nuclear power plants still store their spent fuel on-site, although a spent fuel storage facility at the Lanzhou Nuclear Fuel Complex is available. There are two depositories for low- and intermediate-level radioactive wastes. One is near Yumen in Gansu province and the other at Beilong near the Daya Bay power station. The deep underground geological repository for high-level radioactive wastes is still under development. Three candidate sites have been identified in the Beishan area in Gansu province. (WNA, 2016b)

Chapter highlights

- The Chinese nuclear power industry is dominated by three state-owned corporations.
- The Chinese policymakers' call for standardization has been resisted by state-owned corporations.
- China is building more nuclear power reactors than any other countries.
- The Chinese government has implemented technology indigenization policies to help selected Chinese equipment manufacturers acquire technology and establish manufacturing capability.
- The feed-in tariff and cost-plus pricing of nuclear electricity have guaranteed the profits of nuclear power projects in China.
- NYMBY is hardly an issue in the siting of nuclear projects in China.

Note

1 The China Guangdong Nuclear Power Group was later renamed in 2013 as China General Nuclear Power Group, while keeping the CGN abbreviation and logo.

References

CEC, 2005. *China's Nuclear Power Industry Moves From 'Moderate Development' to 'Accelerate and Push Forward'*. www.cec.org.cn/yaowenkuaidi/2010-11-26/2075. html (in Chinese) (accessed 12/26/2016)

CEC, 2016. *2015 National Power Industry Statistical Table.* China Electricity Council, Beijing (in Chinese: 2015 全国电力工业统计数据一览表, 中国电力企业联合会)

Energy, 2014. *Decoding the Technology Roadmap of 3rd Generation Nuclear Power: Compromised Plan After the Infighting Between CNNC and CGN.* http://business. sohu.com/20140409/n397975604.shtml (in Chinese) (accessed 12/26/2016)

He, Y., 2008. Here comes the nuclear power plant. *China Entrepreneur* 313, 80–86 (in Chinese: 何伊凡,村里要建核电站,中国企业家)

Hook, L., 2012. China nuclear protest picks up steam. *Financial Times*, March 1. www.ftchinese.com/story/001043416/en (accessed 12/27/2016)

IESM, 2014. *Strategy and Keys to Electricity Pricing Reform.* www.china-reform.org/? content_540.html (in Chinese) (accessed 12/27/2016)

Jiang, X., 2011. *Crime and Punishment of Jiangxi Pengze Nuclear Power Station.* www.china5e.com/html/old_special_html/special_510.html (in Chinese) (accessed 12/27/2016)

Lin, C., 2016. *Hualong 1 Internationalization Process Launched; Industry Insider Says Risks Still Exist.* http://business.sohu.com/20160223/n438250242.shtml (in Chinese) (accessed 12/26/2016)

Ma, K. Li, H., Li, C., 2011. China's nuclear power continue to be entangled. *Caijing.* http://magazine.caijing.com.cn/20110411/700958.shtml (in Chinese)(accessed 12/25/2016)

MEP/NEA/CEA, 2012. *Report on Comprehensive Safety Inspection of Civilian Nuclear Facilities.* Ministry of Environmental Protection/National Energy Administration/China Earthquake Administration, Beijing, 2012 (in Chinese: 关于全国民用核设施综合安全检查情况的报告)

MOST, 2010. *China's Installed Power Capacity Reaches 900 Million Kilowatts, Total Capacity Is Second in the World.* Ministry of Science and Technology. www.most.gov.cn/kjbgz/201009/t20100928_82401.htm (in Chinese) (accessed 12/26/2016)

NDRC, 2007. *Nuclear Power Development Medium to Long-Term Development Plan (2005–2020).* National Development and Reform Commission, Beijing (in Chinese: 核电中长期发展规划 (2005–2020))

NEA, 2011. *Roadmap of China's Nuclear Power Equipment Indigenization.* www. nea.gov.cn/2011-06/14/c_131093442.htm (in Chinese) (accessed 12/27/2016)

NEA, 2012. *Energy Development in the 11th Five-Year Plan.* www.gov.cn/test/2012-06/26/content_2169887_2.htm (in Chinese) (accessed 12/25/2016)

Wang, B., 2011. Develop nuclear power highly efficiently on the basis of ensuring safety. *Qiushi.* www.qstheory.cn/zxdk/2011/201106/201103/t20110314_73146. htm (accessed 12/26/2016)

Wen, H., 2007. Insisting on 'two-step' principle, steadily developing nuclear power. *China Nuclear Industry* 79(3), 20–25 (in Chinese: 温鸿钧,坚持 '两步走' 方针 积极稳妥地推进核电发展.中国核工业)

WNA, 2016a. *World Nuclear Power Reactors and Uranium Requirements.* World Nuclear Association. www.world-nuclear.org/information-library/facts-and-figures/world-nuclear-power-reactors-and-uranium-requireme.aspx (accessed 1/5/2017)

WNA, 2016b. *China's Nuclear Fuel Cycle.* www.world-nuclear.org/information-library/country-profiles/countries-a-f/china-nuclear-fuel-cycle.aspx (accessed 12/27/2016)

Zhu, X., 2013. *Nuclear Power Enters the Age of Benchmark Pricing.* http://paper.people.com.cn/zgnyb/html/2013-07/08/content_1266159.htm (in Chinese) (accessed 12/26/2016)

8 Wind power

The wind power industry in China is rather competitive and has many private players. Nevertheless, the Chinese government has actively promoted technology indigenization with domestic content requirements and implemented favorable policies to support its selected winner. Unfortunately, the winner picked by the government did not perform as well as hoped.

The earliest grid-connected wind farms in China were built in the 1980s with foreign grants and loans, as well as imported wind turbines. In the Seventh (1986–1990) and Eighth Five-Year Plans (1991–1995), the government provided funds for the development of indigenous wind turbines. Wind power continued to develop mainly as R&D programs until the early 2000s, when the Chinese central government conceived the concession approach (Wang et al., 2015).

In 2003, the NDRC launched the wind power concession program, where investors were invited to develop two 100-MW wind farms through international competitive bidding. The Chinese government guaranteed feed-in tariffs for the concession projects. The wind power concession program jump-started an explosive growth of wind power industry in China. The central government procured six rounds of concession projects (Table 8.1), which accounted for most of the wind power installations during this period.

The legislation of the Renewable Energy Law in 2005 was generally considered an important milestone in China's commitment to renewable energy. The law itself contains nothing that the State Council cannot do with executive orders, and the legislature (National People's Congress) is little more than a rubber stamp. Nevertheless, this legislation was a high-profile symbolic gesture that declared the suddenly elevated priority of renewable energy in national policy agenda.

With high priority in national agenda, wind power investors soon enjoyed many preferential policies, including tax reduction, subsidies, and technical supports in wind resource surveys, equipment, and component testing and certification. With the successful experiences of feed-in tariffs in the

Table 8.1 Wind power concession program

Round	Year	No. of wind farms	Total capacity
1	2003	2	200 MW
2	2004	5	700 MW
3	2005	3	500 MW
4	2006	4	1000 MW
5	2007	4	950 MW
6	2009	25	5250 MW

Source: Li (2009); Li et al. (2012)

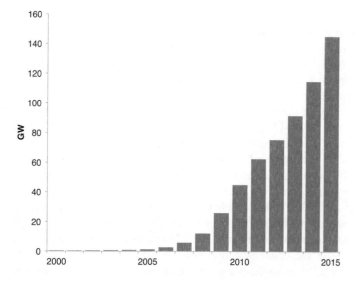

Figure 8.1 Installed wind power capacities in China
Source: BP (2016)

concession program, the NDRC extended the benchmark pricing (feed-in tariffs) to all wind power projects in 2009.

The "Renewable Energy Medium and Long-Term Development Plan," published in 2007, set the wind power installation target at 5 GW for 2010, and 20 GW for 2020. At that time, the targets seemed reasonably ambitious. The goal was to quadruple China's wind power capacity from 2005 to 2010, and quadruple again from 2010 to 2020.

The 2010 target was met in 2007, and the 2020 target was surpassed in 2009 (Figure 8.1). In 2010, the total installed wind power capacity in China surpassed that of the United States, and China's wind power capacity has been the largest in the world since then.

Technology indigenization by domestic content standards

Technology indigenization programs have always been important parts of Chinese energy policy. Wind power is certainly no exception. However, the wind power R&D programs from mid-1980s to mid-1990s had little commercial success. In 1997, the "Ride the Wind" program was launched to form two joint-venture factories with foreign technology providers. Unfortunately, at that time, the Chinese market was not big enough to attract the technology leaders. With little to offer, the "Ride the Wind" program set the local content standard at only 20%. Rapid technology transfer and indigenization did not start until 2003, when the concession program began.

In the first and second rounds of the concession projects, there were only two selection criteria: (1) low electricity price, and (2) high domestic content. In 2005, the selection criteria were revised to be based on a weighted average of multiple indicators, but electricity price and domestic content remained the most important ones (Jiang and Shi, 2006). The domestic content standards of the concession projects were steadily raised from the initial mandate of 50% in 2003, to 70% in 2004, and 75% in 2006 (CWPC, 2006; Lewis, 2007). Based on the successful experiences of the domestic content standards in the concession program, the NDRC extended 70% domestic content standard to all wind farms in China in 2005 (NEA, 2005). In 2009, the Chinese government revoked all domestic content standards for wind power, likely because local content requirements have always been explicitly forbidden by the WTO, which China joined in 2001.

Before 2005, Chinese manufacturers could only assemble wind turbines that were smaller than 0.6 MW and relied on imports for most key components. Foreign suppliers dominated the wind power market in China. With aggressive indigenization programs, Chinese manufacturers quickly built up their capacities and acquired the ability to make larger and larger wind turbines. Chinese makers started to make 0.75-MW turbines in 2005, 1.5-MW turbines in 2006, 2-MW in 2008, and 3-MW by 2010 (Li et al., 2012). Among the Chinese wind turbine makers, Sinovel experienced the most dramatic increase in market shares.

In 2000, foreign wind turbine makers accounted for over 90% of Chinese wind power market. The foreign suppliers' market shares dropped to about 75% by 2004, and roughly 10% by 2010. When the U.S. Trade Representative initiated Section 301 investigation over China's unfair trade practices in the development of its green technologies in 2010, the Chinese government explained that the accusation was based on a misunderstanding because the local content requirements were already revoked. By 2014, only 1.7% of the wind turbines installed in China were made by foreign companies (CWEA, 2016).

Low capacity factors

In hindsight, the peculiarly high-speed growth of wind power capacity in China from 2004 to 2010 (Figure 8.2) might have caused the quality to suffer. A common indicator for the quality of wind turbines is the capacity factor. The capacity factor is defined as the actual electricity output in a period of time divided by the theoretical maximum output if the generators were running at full capacity during the period. Higher capacity factors indicate more reliable and efficient wind turbines. Figure 8.3 compares the annual average capacity factors of wind power in China, Europe, and the United States. Before 2004, when China imported most of its wind turbines, the average capacity factors of wind power in China were comparable to those in Europe and the United States. Since 2004, the performances of wind turbines in China declined quickly. The capacity factors started to rise again after the local content requirements were abolished, but a very significant performance gap has remained.

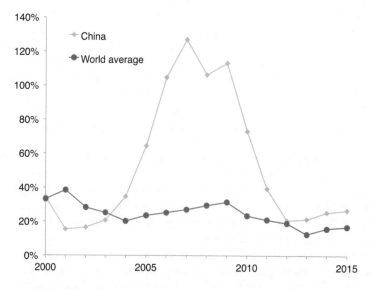

Figure 8.2 Annual growth rates of accumulated wind power capacity
Source: BP (2016)

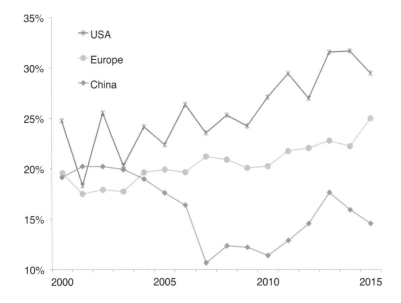

Figure 8.3 Average capacity factors of wind power generators in the United States, Europe, and China

Source: BP (2016)

Rise and fall of Sinovel

Sinovel was established in 2005, and soon won three concession projects in 2006 and more projects in 2007. In December 2007, it was selected as the wind turbine supplier for China's first offshore wind farm demonstration project, with no prior experience in making such wind turbines at all.

Prior to the sudden rise of Sinovel, Gold Wind has long been the largest Chinese wind turbine maker. In 2008, Sinovel suddenly overtook Gold Wind as the leading wind turbine supplier in China, only three years after it was founded (Figure 8.4). Sinovel occupied the largest market share in China from 2008 to 2010. With China's increasing weight in the global wind power business, Sinovel's global market share ranking ascended from the seventh in 2008, to the third in 2009, to the second in 2010. The sudden and dramatic rise of Sinovel as the instant champion of wind power in China was legendary. Han Junliang, founder and chairman of Sinovel, declared in 2009 that Sinovel would become the number one wind turbine maker in the world within five years.

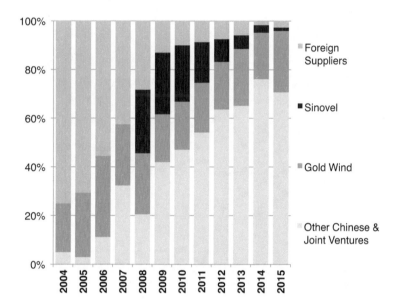

Figure 8.4 Evolution of market shares in annual wind power installations in China
Source: CWEA (2003–2015); CNREC (2015)

The Sinovel legend was built on excellent timing, favorable government policies, and very aggressive strategy. In 2004, Han Junliang licensed the design of a 1.5-MW wind turbine from the German company Fuhrländer. At that time, no Chinese manufacturer had any experience in producing wind turbines that were bigger than 0.75-MW. As soon as the Chinese government started to impose stringent local content requirements, Sinovel became the biggest winner in the concession projects. In 2009, when the Chinese government was procuring the first offshore wind power project, Sinovel was the first one to build two 3-MW prototype offshore wind turbines, even though they failed to function as expected. Chinese policymakers considered the offshore wind farm as a matter of national prestige, and intended to show it off at the Expo 2010 in Shanghai. The most important thing about the offshore wind turbines was that they must be completed in time to look good at the Expo. Whether they can generate enough electricity to be cost-effective was not very important. Sinovel was successful in the timely completion of the Shanghai Donghai Bridge (Offshore) Wind Farm, and the average capacity factor of its first five years of operation was about 23.8% (Zhang, 2016a). For comparison, the average offshore wind power capacity factors were about 42% in Belgium and 47% in Germany during the same period (NREL, 2015).

By giving the Chinese government what it want, Sinovel secured its place as the government's favorite. An anonymous salesperson in Chinese wind power industry mentioned that: "Government officials had more than once brought up the idea of building the 'Vestas' of China, which we all knew they meant Sinovel" (Pu and Yu, 2013).

On January 5 2011, Sinovel had its initial public offering (IPO) at the record-breaking price of 90 RMB per share in the history of Shanghai Stock Exchange. Since then, the share prices and business of Sinovel have been going completely downhill. After a few years of operation, the low quality of Sinovel products has become increasingly known in the industry. The market share of Sinovel shrank from 23.2% in 2010, to 9.3% in 2012, and 3.1% in 2014 (Figure 8.4).

In 2012, Han Junliang stepped down as the chairman of Sinovel. A year later, his successor also resigned. The stock share of Sinovel plummeted from 90 RMB at IPO to less than 2 RMB in 2014. As it turned out, the descent of the instant champion was just as fast as its ascent.

Tax wind to subsidize coal

China started to experience severe surplus of electricity as its economic growth slowed down since 2014. In order to manage the surplus and relieve the financial difficulties of coal-fired power, several provincial governments started to order wind farms to shut down or to buy production quota from coal-fired power plants. Xinjiang autonomous region imposed a levy of 0.2 to 0.25 RMB per kWh on wind power, and used the revenue to support coal-fired power plants. Yunnan province also demanded wind power and hydropower generators to transfer some of their revenues to coal-fired power generators. Gansu province required renewable power generators to sell electricity in competitive direct power purchase deals, which resulted in much lower prices than the feed-in tariffs, while coal-fired generators continued to sell at the higher benchmark prices (feed-in tariffs). In 2016, China Renewable Energy Society announced its intention to file a lawsuit against the governments of Xinjiang, Yunnan, and Gansu for their blatant violations of the Renewable Energy Law (Zhang, 2016b).

Chapter highlights

- The wind power concession program in 2003 jump-started the wind power market in China.
- China has very quickly installed the largest wind power capacity in the world.

- The wind power concession projects required domestic content standards to foster domestic wind turbine manufacturing capacity.
- The capacity factors of wind farms in China are much lower than those in the United States and Europe.
- The winner picked by the Chinese government did not excel as expected in the wind turbine business.
- Facing power surplus, several provincial governments decided to tax wind power to subsidize coal-fired power.

References

BP, 2016. *Statistical Review of World Energy*. BP, London

CNREC, 2015. *Renewable Energy Data Handbook*. China National Renewable Energy Centre, Beijing, China. (in Chinese: 可再生能源数据手册2015) www.cnrec.org.cn/cbw/zh/2015-10-23-488.html (accessed 1/9/2017)

CWEA, 2003–2015. *China Wind Power Installed Capacity Statistics*. China Wind Energy Association. www.cwea.org.cn/download/display_list.asp?cid=9 (in Chinese: 中国风电装机容量统计) (accessed 1/5/2017)

CWEA, 2016. *Evolution of Wind Power Market Competition in China*. China Wind Energy Association. www.china5e.com/news/news-963345-1.html (in Chinese) (accessed 12/29/2016)

CWPC, 2006. *Policy and Regulation*. China Wind Power Center. www.cwpc.cn/cwpp/cn/informationn/wind-power-policy/361/?ccm_paging_p_b278=2 (in Chinese) (accessed 12/29/2016)

Jiang, L.-P., Shi, P.-F., 2006. Implementation situation of wind power concession bidding projects in China and analysis. *Electric Power Technologic Economics* 18(4), 1–4 (in Chinese: 蒋莉萍,施鹏飞,我国风电特许权招标项目实施情况及综合分析,电力技术经济)

Lewis, J.I., 2007. *A Review of the Potential International Trade Implications of Key Wind Power Industry Policies in China*. Energy Foundation China Sustainable Energy Program

Li, J., Gao, H., Wang, Z-Y., Ma, L-J., Dong, L-Y., 2008. *China Wind Power Report 2008*. China Environmental Science Press, Beijing (in Chinese: 李俊峰等, 2008 中国风电发展报告,中国环境科学出版社)

Li, J., Cai, F., Chao, L., Xie, H., Gao, H., Yang, X., Tang, W., Wang, W., Li, X., 2012. *China Wind Power Report 2012*. China Environmental Science Press, Beijing (in Chinese: 李俊峰等, 2012中国风电发展报告,中国环境科学出版社)

Li, X., 2009. *Capacity Is Increasing, Competition Is Enhanced*. Bohai Securities. www.ewww.com.cn/UploadFiles/58414852436b4a248bcd31d20f3aa36f.pdf (in Chinese) (accessed 1/5/2017)

NEA, 2005. *NDRC Notice on the Requirements for Wind Power Construction and Management*. National Energy Administration. www.nea.gov.cn/2005-08/10/c_131052907.htm (in Chinese) (accessed 12/29/2016)

NREL, 2015. *2014–2015 Offshore Wind Technologies Market Report*. National Renewable Energy Laboratory

Pu, J., Yu, N., 2013. The cycle of Sinovel. *Caixin Weekly*, June 28. http://m.magazine. caixin.com/m/2013-06-28/100548513_all.html (in Chinese) (accessed 12/28/2016)

Wang, C., Wang, W., Zhang, L., Qiao, X., 2015. The analysis of China wind power industry. *Journal of Chongqing University* 38(1), 148–154 (in Chinese: 王长路, 王伟功,张立勇,乔雪涛,中国风电产业发展分析,重庆大学学报)

Zhang, Y., 2016a. Wind industry protest 'abandon wind to save thermal'. *Caixin Weekly*, April 15. http://weekly.caixin.com/2016-04-15/100932361.html (in Chinese) (accessed 1/3/2017)

Zhang, Z., 2016b. Exploring the Chinese path to offshore wind power. *China Energy News*, June 13. http://paper.people.com.cn/zgnyb/html/2016-06/13/content_ 1687660.htm (in Chinese) (accessed 1/3/2017)

9 Solar energy

The rise of China in photovoltaic (PV) manufacturing and installation has been a global spectacle. The rise started with PV manufacturing for export. China's PV manufacturing industry has expanded at astonishing speed since the mid-2000s, and has established itself as the largest in the world since 2009. The domestic installation of PV power did not take off until around 2009, but has been skyrocketing since then. In 2015, China has surpassed Germany as the country of the largest installed PV power capacity.

However, the full scope of solar energy encompasses more than just PV. Solar water heaters have indeed produced much more useful energy than PV in China. The promotion of solar energy in China started in the 1970s during the Oil Crisis. However, the solar energy technology was rather inefficient and unreliable at that time. Those solar energy products were quickly abandoned. Widespread adoption of solar energy did not occurred in China until the late 1990s, when solar water heaters became increasingly popular.

Solar water heater

The adoption of solar water heaters was largely driven by market demand, because solar water heaters indeed offered a clean, convenient, and cost-effective way to make hot water. By the mid-2000s, China has become the largest market of solar water heaters, accounting for over 60% of global installed capacity. In 2007, the NDRC started to mandate installation of solar water heaters in hospitals, schools, hotels, swimming pools, and other major hot water users, and incorporated the design of solar water heaters into building codes. The continued promotion has secured China's leading role in solar water heating. By the end of 2015, China has installed 320 thermal GW of solar water heaters, which accounted for 71% of global capacity (REN21, 2016).

From a technical perspective, the adoption of solar water heating in China has by far greater contribution in greenhouse gas mitigation than PV, but has received by far less attention in the discourses of climate policy. This might be because solar water heaters are simple and mature technology, which is much less glamorous than the fancy high-tech PV technology.

Photovoltaic

From the late 1960s to the 1970s, a Chinese research institute had conducted research and produced small amount of photovoltaic (PV) panels for its satellites. In the 1980s, several PV production lines were established. The production volume remained very small. By 2002, China's total annual PV output was only 2 MWp.

Rise of Suntech and Chinese PV makers

In 2001, Suntech Power was established with US$6 million provided by the Wuxi city government. It immediately started to build China's first 10-MWp PV cell production line, which suddenly quadrupled China's total PV manufacturing capacity. From 2003 to 2005, Suntech contributed to more than half of all PV production in China, and the company quickly ascended to a legendary status (Stokes, 2012; Brown, 2015). On December 14 2005, Suntech had its initial public offering (IPO) at the New York Stock Exchange (NYSE) (Cowan, 2005), and its market capitalization jumped to about US$3.8 billion by the end of that day.

The IPO suddenly made Mr. Shi Zhengrong, founder and chairman of Suntech, the richest man in China. There was a plethora of media coverage of his success stories. For example, the *China Entrepreneur* magazine had a cover story entitled "New richest man, made by government" to introduce Shi and his Suntech (He, 2013). It was clear that the Suntech success had a lot to do with the favorable government policies, including easy access to loans from state-owned banks.

Following Suntech's ascent to glory, Chinese investors rushed into the PV manufacturing business, and founded many companies. Most notably, the JA Solar was founded in 2005, Yingli Green Energy, LDK Solar, and Trina Solar in 2006, and JinkoSolar in 2007. By the end of 2007, there were more than 50 PV manufacturing companies in China. Every province and autonomous region has prioritized PV industries as its strategic industry. All these PV startups enjoyed favorable policies and expanded very quickly.

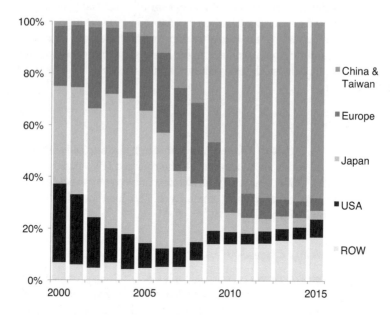

Figure 9.1 PV module production by region
Source: Fraunhofer ISE (2016)

Chinese PV manufacturers quickly increased their production, which were mainly for exports. The growth of their market shares was truly phenomenal (Figure 9.1). Within just a few years, Chinese makers grew from insignificant suppliers to the most dominant ones.

There were several keys to the Chinese PV makers' success: excellent timing, favorable government policies, easy finance, and aggressive strategy. These companies entered the market when there was sustained shortage. The demand for PV products exceeded the suppliers' ability to produce, and the prices were rising (Figure 9.2). Favorable government policies enabled them to acquire the funding and avoided bureaucratic delays so they could build their production lines much faster than their competitors in other countries. By reacting quickly to market demand and investing bravely, Chinese PV makers captured more than 60% of the global PV market.

With extremely aggressive expansion strategy, including borrowing heavily and building production lines very quickly, Suntech sudden became the fourth largest PV manufacturer in the world in 2006, the third in 2007 and 2008, the second in 2009, and finally the number one in the world in 2010 and 2011.

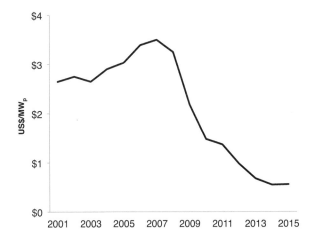

Figure 9.2 PV module price trend

Source: Mints (2012); Schachinger (2016)

Golden Sun demonstration

In 2009, when the PV prices were dropping quickly (Figure 9.2) and the Chinese PV makers were starting to have financial troubles, the Ministry of Finance, the Ministry of Technology, and the National Energy Administration jointly announced the "Golden Sun" demonstration program. The purpose was to create a domestic market for the Chinese PV makers. The "Golden Sun" program provided lump sum subsidies to PV power generation projects upon the approvals of the applications.

Some recipients took the money and disappeared, and some repurposed the money. For those who actually used the money to build PV projects, they tend to choose the cheapest equipment to save money. An anonymous businessman described: "Many enterprises rushed to it. They were obsessed like it was a lottery. Those who got approved were like winning a lottery, and the chance of winning was pretty high." Many of the PV farms were built with no intention to generate power at all. They were only built so the recipients could have something to show the government. In 2012, among the 354 Golden Sun projects within the SGCC service territory, only 157 applied for grid connection (Xinhuanet, 2013).

In 2013, the Chinese government decided to terminate the Golden Sun program and started to audit the projects and investigate for frauds. The Ministry of Finance was reportedly seeking to retrieve subsidies from 80% of the projects.

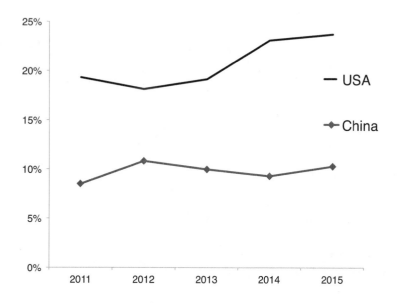

Figure 9.3 Capacity factors of PV in China and grid-scale PV in the United States
Source: BP (2016); USEIA (2016)

The Golden Sun approach likely had contributed to the low capacity factors of China's PV farms. Figure 9.3 compares the capacity factors of Chinese PV generators, which are predominantly grid-scale, and those of grid-scale PV generators in the United States. The outputs of grid-scale PV generators in China were about half of those in the United States.

Suntech bankruptcy

The strategy of aggressive expansion with high financial leverage (i.e., heavy borrowing) worked extremely well when the market was in short supply. However, with many new entrants all expanding quickly, the market was gradually saturated, and the prices of PV modules started to fall after 2007 (Figure 9.2). Facing increasingly oversupplied markets, Suntech chose a very risky and aggressive approach, which was to double down on its expansion plan. It captured even greater market shares from 2008 to 2010 by sacrificing its profit.

To be fair, most people have believed that the overall PV industry is going to have a very bright future. The question is which manufacturers are going to survive until that future arrives. Securing its status as the world's largest PV manufacturer and making it too big to fail might have been the survival strategy of Suntech. Unfortunately, the Wuxi city government was not prepared to bail out Suntech unconditionally. After the negotiation between Suntech and the Wuxi city government failed, Suntech declared bankruptcy in 2013.

The United States started to impose antidumping duty on Chinese PV products in 2012, and the European Union started in 2013. The antidumping taxes further made the business environment even more difficult for Chinese PV makers.

After the fall of Suntech, Yingli Green Energy became the world's largest PV maker in 2012 and 2013, and Trina Solar took over as the largest in 2014 and 2015. Another major Chinese PV maker LDK solar went bankrupt in 2015. Both Yingli and Trina have also suffered heavy financial losses, but have managed to avoid bankruptcy so far, at least until the time this book is written.

The winners picked by the Chinese government in the PV industry have not performed as well as those in the nuclear power and hydropower industry. Perhaps a major difference is that the Chinese government controls the markets of nuclear and hydropower, but not the PV market. The Chinese PV industry has primarily depended on exports. Figure 9.4 shows the ratios

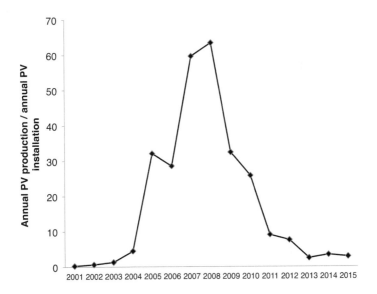

Figure 9.4 Annual PV production/annual PV installation in China

Source: Earth Institute (2015)

between China's annual PV production and its annual installed capacities. From 2005 to 2010, Chinese PV makers produced over 20 times more than their domestic sales. After China ramped up its PV installation, the ratio dropped significantly after 2013. The greatly expanded domestic market will likely be a great help to the Chinese PV makers.

Rooftop PV

As early as 2002, the Chinese government had included the installation of distributed PV systems in its rural electrification program, but the installed capacities were very limited. Many local governments have also implemented their rooftop PV programs with very limited success.

For example, in 2005, the Shanghai city government launched the "100,000 Rooftop Solar Energy" program, which aimed to install 10,000 rooftop PV systems by 2010, and 100,000 by 2015. Prof. Zhao Chuanjiang of Shanghai University of Electric Power was the first one to install a rooftop PV system in Shanghai. In 2006, his rooftop PV system started to generate more than enough power for his family's consumption, so the surplus was fed into the power grid. Unfortunately, at that time, the grid company only provided meters that could not tell the direction of electric currents. No matter whether the electricity was going in or out, the reading from the meter would only go up. Not only he could not get any payment from the grid; he in fact was charged for the electricity he sent to the grid. The problem remained unsolved for five years, while Prof. Zhao's rooftop PV remained the only one in Shanghai.

In 2011, the grid company replaced his meter with a smart one that could distinguish the direction of the current. Unfortunately, he was informed that the feed-in tariff for rooftop PV was not yet determined, so he still would not be paid for the electricity he fed into the grid. At least he no longer had to pay to donate electricity to the power grid. His problem was not resolved until 2014 (Hong, 2013; Ma, 2013; Zhu, 2013).

As previously mentioned in Chapter 5, the grid companies in China are powerful organizations who do not always follow government policies. They generally appeared not very supportive of rooftop PV. As a result, the adoption of rooftop PV in China has been much slower than utility-scale PV.

In 2013, the Chinese government started to pay more attention to distributed PV installation and provided an additional subsidy for distributed PV. Since then, the installation of distributed PV has accelerated. At the end of 2015, the nationwide grid-connected distributed PV capacity has reached 6 GW, which accounted for about 14% of total PV capacity in China.

Chapter highlights

- China is the global leader in using solar water heaters, which generate far more clean energy than photovoltaic.
- Good timing, favorable government policies, and aggressive expansion strategy were the keys to the rise of Chinese PV manufacturers.
- Although the installed PV capacities are high in China, their power outputs are low.
- The development of distributed PV has been less successful than utility-scale PV in China.

References

BP, 2016. *Statistical Review of World Energy*. BP, London

Brown, L.R., 2015. *The Great Transition: Shifting From Fossil Fuels to Solar and Wind Energy*. W. W. Norton & Company. Supporting data: www.earth-policy.org/data_center/C23 (accessed 12/30/2016)

Cowan, L., 2005. Suntech Power IPO jumps 41%. *The Wall Street Journal*, December 15. www.wsj.com/articles/SB113461683329123143 (accessed 12/30/2016)

Earth Institute, 2015. *Annual Solar Photovoltaics Cell Production by Country*. www.earth-policy.org/data_center/C23 (accessed 1/5/2017)

Fraunhofer ISE, 2016. *Photovoltaics Report*. Fraunhofer Institute for Solar Energy Systems, Freiburg, Germany

He, Y., 2013. New richest man, made by government. *China Entrepreneur*, March 20. www.iceo.com.cn/renwu2013/2013/0321/265279.shtml (in Chinese) (accessed 12/30/2016)

Hong, W., 2013. Why is the development of distributed power stations delayed? *New York Time*, July 23. http://cn.nytimes.com/business/20130723/cc23solar/ (in Chinese) (accessed 12/30/2016)

Ma, Y., 2013. *The First Rooftop Solar Person Signed Power Purchase Contract With Electricity Department*. www.chinanews.com/sh/2013/07-31/5108167.shtml (in Chinese) (accessed 12/30/2016)

Mints, P., 2012. *The Solar PV Ecosystem, a Brief History and a Look Ahead*. www.renewableenergyworld.com/articles/2012/11/the-solar-pv-ecosystem-a-brief-history-and-a-look-ahead.html (accessed 1/5/2017)

REN21, 2016. *Renewables 2016 Global Status Report*. Renewable Energy Policy Network for the 21st Century, Paris

Schachinger, M., 2016. Module price index. *PV Magazine*. www.pv-magazine.com/features/investors/module-price-index/ (accessed 1/5/2017)

Stokes, J., 2012. *Global PV Markets: Dynamics, Competition, Benefits*. Suntech Power International Ltd

USEIA, 2016. *Utility-Scale Solar Electricity Net Generation and EIA-860 Database.* U.S. Energy Information Administration

Xinhuanet, 2013. *Golden Sun Program Formally Ends in this Year; Widely Criticized for Prevalent Frauds.* http://news.xinhuanet.com/2013-10/10/c_125504749.htm (in Chinese) (accessed 12/30/2016)

Zhu, J., 2013. *PV Power Sales Encounter Difficulties, Prospect of Household PV Power Generation Unclear.* http://finance.people.com.cn/n/2013/0731/c1004-22386491.html (in Chinese) (accessed 12/30/2016)

10 Biomass

The development of biomass energy is much less successful than most other renewable energy resources in China. Among the five targets for biomass energy in the 11th Five-Year Plan (2005–2010), three were not met (Table 10.1). In the 12th Five-Year Plan (2011–2015), all the five targets were missed (Table 10.2). Biomass constitutes only a tiny share in Chinese energy economy. It accounted for 0.67% of total primary energy consumption in 2010 and 0.81% in 2015.

Table 10.1 Biomass energy targets and results in the 11th Five-Year Plan

	2010 target	*2010 result*	*Unit*
Biomass-fired power capacity	5.5	5.5	GW
Biogas	19	14	billion cubic meters
Biomass pellet fuel	1	0.5	million metric tons
Non-food bio-ethanol	2	1.8	million metric tons
Biodiesel	0.2	0.5	million metric tons

Table 10.2 Biomass energy targets and results in the 12th Five-Year Plan

	2015 target	*2015 result*	*Unit*
Biomass-fired power capacity	13	10.3	GW
Biogas	22	19	billion cubic meters
Biomass pellet fuel	10	8	million metric tons
Non-food bio-ethanol	4	2.1	million metric tons
Biodiesel	1	0.8	million metric tons

Biomass pellet/biomass-fired electricity

In 2008, the Ministry of Finance started to provide subsidies to biomass pellet fuel projects. Many small enterprises applied and received financial supports. The Ministry of Finance soon discovered many falsified invoices, receipts, and forged sales statistics. In 2013, the subsidy was suspended. In 2015, the subsidy scheme was officially abolished.

Because the supply of biomass pellet fuels is not always reliable and the biomass fuels are more expensive than coal, many biomass power generators use coal as supplement or replacement, while selling electricity as renewable to take advantage of the higher feed-in tariffs. Compared to large coal-fired power plants, the biomass power generators are smaller and less efficient, with no or less sophisticated emission control device. When biomass burners use coal as fuel, they are indeed dirtier than regular coal-fired power plants. Over time, biomass-fired power has been labeled as "dirty energy." Chinese policymakers appear undecided about whether to continue the support for biomass-fired electricity or not (Xiao, 2015).

Biogas

Biogas is the most successful part of biomass energy in China. Since the early 2000s, the central government has been providing financial supports to biogas projects as a part of its rural development program. From 2003 to 2008, the number of rural households with biogas pond increased from 11.1 million to 30.5 million. Professional service networks have been established to provide repairs and maintenance to the biogas systems (Li and Xue, 2000).

By 2010, the rural households with biogas have increased to 40 million, and livestock and poultry farms have installed more than 50,000 industrial biogas systems. During the 12th Five-Year Plan (2011–2015), the growth of household-scale biogas has slowed down, while industrial biogas systems became increasingly popular. At the end of 2015, there were 43.8 million household biogas systems and more than 100,000 industrial biogas systems in China (NEA, 2016).

Bio-ethanol and biodiesel

In the 10th Five-Year Plan (2001–2005), the Chinese government started to develop bio-ethanol fuel. In 2001, four state-owned bio-ethanol enterprises were established to produce ethanol from expired grain (wheat and corn) stocks. A few private companies also started to make biodiesel since 2001. By 2006, there were 25 biodiesel companies, with combined annual capacity of 1.2 million metric tons. However, the actual production was only 0.5 million metric tons by 2010. The overly aggressive expansion strategy and low capacity utilization seemed to be a very prevalent phenomenon in China.

Due to the concern over food security, Chinese policymakers started to emphasize non-food bio-fuels since the 11th Five-Year Plan. There have been many R&D and demonstration projects on non-food bio-fuel, but the outputs were rather limited. In the 12th Five-Year Plan, both targets for bio-ethanol and biodiesel were missed (NDRC, 2008).

The 13th Five-Year Plan (2015–2020) set the targets for 2020 as four million metric tons for bio-ethanol and two million for biodiesel. With much lower petroleum prices since 2014, these targets seem very ambitious.

Garbage incineration

As China becomes increasingly urbanized, garbage disposal is increasingly challenging almost everywhere. Many landfills are quickly running out of space. Garbage incineration seems to be a reasonable option.

Since the early 2000s, many Chinese cities have been building garbage incinerators, and many of them are equipped with power generators to utilize the heat. The NDRC started to provide a subsidy to the feed-in tariffs of electricity from garbage incinerators since 2006.

Because the heat content of garbage in China is often too low to sustain a satisfactory temperature in the incinerators, the operators typically blend coal into the garbage. The subsidized feed-in tariffs for garbage incinerators are more than enough to cover the cost of coal. The more coal is blended in garbage, the more lucrative the incinerator will be. Therefore, operators of garbage incinerators started to blend more and more coal into garbage (Wu, 2012).

In 2012, the NDRC revised its rules on the feed-in tariffs of garbage-derived electricity. The incinerators that burn more coal than garbage are no longer entitled to the subsidized feed-in tariff. The new rule also caps the allowed electricity output from each ton of garbage to limit coal blending (NDRC, 2012).

The garbage incineration industry has been growing rapidly. The number of garbage incinerators increased from 37 in 2005, to 97 in 2010, and to 220 in 2015. By 2015, garbage incinerators have installed 4.7 GW of power generators (NEA, 2016). The rapid growth is expected to continue in the coming years.

Chapter highlights

- The development of biomass is not as successful as other renewable energy in China.
- Biomass targets in Five-Year Plans were repeatedly missed.
- Coal blending in biomass has jeopardized the legitimacy of biomass as a clean energy.

References

Li, J., Xue, M., 2000. Review and prospect on biogas development in China. *Renewable Energy Resources* 28(3), 1–5 (in Chinese: 李景明,薛梅, 中国沼气产业发展的回顾与展望,可再生能源)

NDRC, 2008. *The Current Implementation and Review of Biological Liquid Fuel Policies in China*. Renewable Energy Development Center, National Development and Reform Commission, Beijing (in Chinese: 国家发展和改革委员会,中国生物液体燃料现行政策的实施与回顾,可再生能源发展中心)

NDRC, 2012. *Notice on Improving Garbage Incineration Power Pricing Policy*. National Development and Reform Commission, Beijing. www.sdpc.gov.cn/fzgggz/jggl/zcfg/201204/t20120410_472400.html (in Chinese) (accessed 1/5/2017)

NEA, 2016. *13th Five-Year Plan for Biomass Energy Development*. National Energy Administration, Beijing (in Chinese: 生物质能发展 '十三五' 规划)

Wu, Y., 2012. *Adjust Subsidy Model, Suppress Coal as Garbage*. http://news.solidwaste.com.cn/view/id_38859 (in Chinese) (accessed 1/5/2017)

Xiao, Q., 2015. Why is biomass pellet fuel abandoned? *China Energy News*, May 11. http://paper.people.com.cn/zgnyb/html/2015-05/11/content_1563953.htm (in Chinese) (accessed 1/1/2017)

11 Energy and environment

The use of energy is a major cause of environmental problems. However, the overlap between energy and environmental policy is a fairly recent phenomenon in China. Before the mid-1990s, environmental policy and energy policy were largely two separate issues in China.

Early years

China had almost no environmental policy before the 1980s. From the First to the Fifth Five-Year Plans (1953–1980), the national policymakers single-mindedly focused on industrialization. The energy policy goal was to increase supply as much as possible, with hardly any consideration on environmental impacts (Ho, 2010). There was no environmental target in the earliest five Five-Year Plans (Bu, 2009).

The Sixth Five-Year Plan (1981–1985) was the first to mention environmental protection. It included a chapter on environmental protection, which briefly and vaguely acknowledged the importance of protecting the environment, but there was no specific goal and no implementation plan. The Seventh Five-Year Plan (1986–1990) established a quantitative goal, which was to bringing about 50% to 70% of industrial pollutions to be in compliance with national standards. Because there was no national standard for most pollutants at that time, this target was rather meaningless. Although the Chinese government claimed to have fulfilled its environmental targets in the Sixth and Seventh Five-Year Plans, this meant hardly any real improvement of environmental quality (Wang, 2009).

Nevertheless, many environmental laws, including the Marine Environment Protection Law, Water Pollution Control Law, Air Pollution Control Law, Forest Law, Grassland Law, Fisheries Law, Water Law, and Wildlife Protection Law were legislated in the 1980s, and the State Environmental Protection Administration was established in 1984.

The Eighth Five-Year Plan (1991–1995) aimed to limit national total smoke emissions to 14 million tons and industrial dust emissions to 7 million tons, and to increase the industrial air emissions treatment rate to 74% and industrial waste comprehensive utilization rate to 33%. In the final assessment of the Eighth Five-Year Plan, the State Planning Commission only vaguely stated that the works on environmental protection and pollution treatment were strengthened (Xin, 1996). Despite the official claim that most environmental targets were met, the overall environmental conditions continued to deteriorate (Zhang and Ma, 1996). The environmental targets in these Five-Year Plan were little more than empty gestures.

The Ninth Five-Year Plan (1996–2000) was the first to tie environmental policy to energy policy to reduce acid rains and sulfur dioxide (SO_2) emissions. The government designated six priority regions for the policy. These six regions were referred to as "Two Control Zones" (Hao et al., 2000). The "Two Control Zones" policy was the most high-profile environmental policy in China at that time. The Chinese government claimed to have successfully met its acid rains and SO_2 targets in the Ninth Five-Year Plan. However, the success was somewhat fortuitous because China's total coal consumption declined during this period, which was most likely a result of the 1997 Asian Financial Crisis.

Strengthened emphasis since 2000

The 10th Five-Year Plan (2000–2005) was a major turning point in China's environmental governance and national planning. It added two high-profile energy and environmental targets: 15%–17% reduction of energy intensity per Gross Domestic Product (GDP), and 10% reduction of major pollutants. The reduction of SO_2 emissions and acid rains remained highly emphasized in the 10th Five-Year Plan (Schreifels et al., 2012). In 2006, Premier Wen Jiabao openly admitted that the environmental targets in the 10th Five-Year Plan were outright failures (Gu and Wu, 2006). The energy intensity per GDP was increased by 27%, national total SO_2 emissions increased by 28%, and total Chemical Oxygen Demand (COD) in wastewater discharges reduced only by 2%. The open acknowledgement of failure was a momentous event. It demonstrated not only the attempt to improve transparency in environmental governance, but also the elevated status of environmental goals in national policy agenda.

Before the 10th Five-Year Plan, the Chinese government typically set ambiguous environmental targets with low transparency in their measurement, and claimed that all the targets were met, even though the environmental quality continued to get worse. Without the willingness to admit failure, the targets were mostly empty promises. The acknowledgement of failure was the first step in making changes. By learning from previous failures, Chinese policymakers adopted several changes in their goal-setting and implementation mechanisms.

Since the 11th Five-Year Plan (2006–2010), the environmental targets became more focused, clearly defined, verifiable, and legally binding. The 11th Five-Year Plan declared eight targets to be legally binding (Table 11.1). One of the most emphasized targets was to reduce per GDP energy consumption by 20%. The national target was further decomposed into local targets for each and every province, city, and county. The local officials were responsible for meeting their designated targets.

Premier Wen Jiabao repeatedly emphasized the importance of meeting the mandatory targets. The attainment of energy and environmental targets was for the first time included in local officials' performance review (Liu and Diamond, 2008). Both the State Council and the Communist Party made it clear that failure of achieving a region's environmental targets would result in a failed evaluation of the local officials.

Despite the repeated information campaigns, not all local officials took the energy intensity target seriously. By the end of 2010, facing impending final performance review of the 11th Five-Year Plan, many local officials resorted to desperate measures to meet their targets.

For example, Anping County in Hebei province implemented a plan of rotational blackout to reduce electricity consumption. Local commercial and residential districts endured 22 hours of blackouts every three days. The local government even cut the power to hospitals and traffic lights to save energy (Jia, 2010).

Similar blackout energy-saving strategies occurred in many places (Tien, 2011). Jincheng city in Shanxi province shut down residential power supply for 14 days within a month. The power rationing scheme at Chuanjiao county in Anhui province forced hospitals to operate with emergency backup generators. Zaoqiang county in Hebei province reduced its residential power supply to only 4 hours per day. The ridiculous energy-saving schemes quickly triggered a wave of criticisms in Chinese media. The NDRC criticized the blackout energy-saving measures, and the local governments soon restored their power supplies. These events, nevertheless, showed that the central government had indeed pressed hard on local officials to achieve energy saving and environmental targets.

Although not all local governments met their energy and environmental targets, on the national scale, the environmental targets in the 11th Five-Year

Plan were successfully met. The experiences in the 11th Five-Year Plan demonstrated the improved effectiveness of the Five-Year Plan approach in energy and environmental governance.

A shift in policy priorities occurred in this period. The Chinese government started to prioritize environmental protection over economic growth, or at least nominally. Both the 11th and 12th (2011–2015) Five-Year Plans designated all environmental targets as binding, and those of economic growth as non-binding (Table 11.1).

Table 11.1 Key targets in the 11th and 12th Five-Year Plans

Targets	2010	2015	Property
Nine-year compulsory education (%)	89.7	93	Binding
Agricultural land (100 million Mu)[1]	18.18	18.18	Binding
Non-fossil energy in primary energy consumption (%)	8.3	11.4	Binding
Per GDP energy consumption (%)	−20	−16	Binding
Per GDP CO_2 emissions reduction (%)	n.a.	−17	Binding
Forest coverage (%)	20.36	21.66	Binding
Urban registered unemployment rate (%)	n.a.	4.1	Binding
Urban participants in pension insurance (100 million persons)	2.57	3.57	Binding
Urban affordable housing (10,000 set)	n.a.	3,600	Binding
Population (10,000 persons)	136,000	134,100	Binding
Reduction of major pollutants: COD, SO_2, ammonia, NO_X (%)	−10	−8–10	Binding
Reduction of water consumption per unit industrial output (%)	n.a.	−30	Binding
GDP (trillion yuan)	39.8	55.8	Non-binding
Percentage of service industry's added value (%)	43	47	Non-binding
Urbanization rate (%)	47.5	51.5	Non-binding
New urban employment (10,000 persons)	n.a.	4,500	Non-binding
Per capita disposable income of urban residents (yuan)	19,109	26,810	Non-binding
Per capita net income of rural resident (yuan)	5,919	8,310	Non-binding
R&D expenditure in GDP (%)	1.8	2.2	Non-binding

The 12th Five-Year Plan (2011–2015) was the first to include a target for CO_2. Like other targets, the national CO_2 intensity target was decomposed into assigned local responsibilities. The target-responsibility system has become an important instrument in energy and climate policy in China. The energy and CO_2 targets in the 12th Five-Year Plan were more than fulfilled. By the end of 2015, China's per GDP energy consumption was reduced by 18.2% and per GDP CO_2 emissions reduced by 20% (Xinhuanet, 2016).

The 13th Five-Year Plan

The 13th Five-Year Plan will continue to reduce energy and CO_2 intensity, and increase the shares of non-fossil energy in primary energy mix (Table 11.2). As long as the national leaders continue to emphasize these goals, the target-responsibility system will push local officials and state-owned companies to work toward achieving the goals.

Table 11.2 Key energy and environmental targets in the 13th Five-Year Plan

Targets	2020	Increase	Property
Agricultural land (100 million Mu)	18.65		Binding
New construction land (10,000 Mu)		<3256	Binding
Per GDP water consumption (%)		−23	Binding
Per GDP energy consumption (%)		−15	Binding
Non-fossil energy in primary energy consumption (%)	15	+3	Binding
Per GDP CO_2 emissions reduction (%)		−18	Binding
Forest coverage (%)	23.04		Binding
Forest stock (100 million cubic meters)	165	+14	Binding
Good air quality days in major cities (%)	>80		Binding
$PM_{2.5}$ concentration reduction in major non-complying cities (%)		−18	Binding
Category III or above surface water bodies (%)	>70		Binding
Category V or worse surface water bodies (%)	<5		Binding
Reduction of COD (%)		−10	Binding
Reduction of ammonia (%)		−10	Binding
Reduction of SO_2 (%)		−15	Binding
Reduction of NO_X (%)		−15	Binding

Chapter highlights

- Energy policy and environmental policy have become increasingly intertwined in recent years.
- The effectiveness of energy and environmental governance in Five-Year Plans has improved over time.
- Reducing energy and carbon intensities have become high-profile priorities in China's national policy agenda.

Note

1 One Chinese "Mu" is 666.67 square meters.

References

Bu, N., 2009. *Development Planning and Environmental Protection.* Shandong University Press, Jinan, China (in Chinese: 布娜, 发展规划与环境保护.山东大学出版社)

Gu, R., Wu, J., 2006. *11th Five-Year Plan Binding Environmental Target Testing the Government's Enforcement.* http://news.xinhuanet.com/environment/2006-04/21/content_4455145.htm (in Chinese) (accessed 2/9/2017)

Hao, J., Wang, S., Liu, B., He, K., 2000. Designation of acid rain and SO_2 control zones and control policies in China. *Journal of Environmental Science and Health, Part A* 35, 1901–1914

Ho, A., 2010. The three shifts in development orientation: Review and prospective of the eleven five-year plans. *Soochow Academic* 3, 74–82 (in Chinese: 何爱国, 发展取向的三次转型:十一个五年规划的回顾与前瞻. 东吴学术)

Jia, Y., 2010. *Anping Hebei Cut Power to All; Local Government Claim to Meet Environmental Target.* http://politics.people.com.cn/BIG5/14562/12641200.html (in Chinese) (accessed 2/9/2017)

Liu, J.G., Diamond, J., 2008. Science and government – Revolutionizing China's environmental protection. *Science* 319, 37–38

Schreifels, J.J., Fu, Y., Wilson, E.J., 2012. Sulfur dioxide control in China: Policy evolution during the 10th and 11th five-year plans and lessons for the future. *Energy Policy* 48, 779–789

Tien, G., 2011. *NDRC Chairman Zhang Ping Respond to Power Cut: Inappropriate Measure, I Will Self-Criticize.* http://cpc.people.com.cn/GB/64093/64102/14078267.html (in Chinese) (accessed 2/9/2017)

Wang, J., 2009. Thirty years' rule of environmental law in China: Retrospect and reassessment. *Journal of China University of Geosciences* (Social Sciences Edition) 9, 3–9 (in Chinese: 汪劲, 中國環境法治三十年:回顧與反思. 中國地質大學學報 (社會科學版))

Xin, R.-Z., 1996. The historical achievements in socioeconomic development during the 8th five-year-plan period. *Economic Reform and Development* 5, 15–18 (in Chinese: 辛仁周, 第八个五年计画时期社会经济发展的历史性成就.经济改革与发展)

Xinhuanet, 2016. *13th Five-Year Plan Outlines*. http://sh.xinhuanet.com/2016-03/18/c_135200400.htm (in Chinese) (accessed 2/9/2017)

Zhang, J., Ma, A., 1996. The main achievements, problems, and 9th five-year-plan strategies in China's environmental protection. *Management World Bimonthly* 4, 208–215 (in Chinese: 张建平, 马爱民, 我国环境保护的主要成就、问题与"九五"对策. 管理世界双月刊)

12 Conclusions

It is not easy to draw any overarching conclusion from such complex and multifaceted stories. China is very unique in the way its government functions and how the various levels of government are involved so directly and prevalently in the energy business, even though most of the Chinese economy has become market-driven. The energy sector is particularly complex, with varying degrees of government control, state-owned company dominance, and different market structure and regulations. This book is mainly to tell the true stories of what happened in China's energy sector, so the readers may draw their own conclusions.

This book contains plenty of evidence that appears to confirm the theory of fragmented authoritarianism. For example, the government demonstrated great power in silencing dissidents in involuntary resettlement and suppressing local opposition to nuclear power sites, but appeared rather powerless when it tried to standardize nuclear reactors and to enforce mining safety regulations. In general, individuals are usually powerless vis-à-vis the state, while different parts of the state can often resist or fight each other.

Although the Chinese government does not separate the legislative, executive, and judicial powers like most Western democracies, checks and balances do happen in some very interesting and peculiar ways. For example, when the state-owned power grid attempted to merge the four networks, its power was checked by the also state-owned telecommunication companies, and the Communist Party does investigate and punish corrupted officials from time to time. Nevertheless, without democratically elected legislature and independent courts, the checks and balances are clearly inadequate.

Unchecked state power (i.e., authoritarianism) has its advantages in some cases. For example, the siting of infrastructure projects in China is usually free from the NYMBY opposition. This unique strength allows China to build and improve its energy infrastructure very quickly. For example, the siting of a new transmission line usually require years and sometimes over a decade in the United States, but only takes about three months in China. Of course, the political realty that the state owns everyone's backyard makes it very convenient for the developers, especially if they are state-owned or state-favored.

The manifestation of the authoritarian power can be good or bad, or a mixture of both. When the Wuxi city government used its power to sponsor Suntech, it successfully created the world champion in PV manufacturing within just a few years. When the state-owned grid company ignored the rooftop PV enthusiast, it also took many years to overcome the bureaucratic hurdles. The state grid corporations have very quickly built the world's largest and strongest interconnected smart power grids, and their generous investment in pumped hydroelectric energy storage will help accommodate more clean energy, but their other ambitions might sometimes seem excessive.

The Chinese government has picked and created many winners in the energy business very quickly, but some of the winners collapsed just as fast as they arose, especially when the government cannot guarantee the markets. Over time, the Chinese economy and industries have become more market-driven and competitive. The Chinese government has also evolved and must continue to adapt to the changing world. The government has made many mistakes, but it also has demonstrated the ability to correct them.

The Chinese people have demonstrated their entrepreneurship and have flourished in the market economy. Their profit-seeking behavior is a mixed blessing. When the world demanded more PV panels than the producers could supply, they seized that opportunity and quickly built the biggest PV industry in the world. When there was a loophole in China's garbage incineration policy, they also quickly seized the opportunity by blending a lot of coal into garbage.

Over time, the Chinese central government has improved its energy and environmental governance and established its vision of transition to a low-carbon economy. However, this low-carbon vision is not completely shared by all local officials and state-owned corporations. Several provincial governments have blatantly violated the Renewable Energy Law when they taxed wind power to subsidize coal-fired electricity. Many companies are still actively pursuing the development of coal conversion industries, which are even more carbon-intensive than coal-fired power. When we categorize energy resources and technologies according to their carbon intensities (Figure 12.1), we find that China is the global leader on not only both ends but also the middle of spectrum. China is simultaneously pursuing multiple paths that lead to low-carbon, high-carbon, and ultra-high-carbon economies.

Some readers may like me to be more forward-looking and want to predict where China is going. The most honest answer I can give is that I don't

Ultra-high-carbon		High-carbon			Low-carbon
Coal-to-liquid Coal-to-olefins	SNG Coal-to-methanol	Coal-fired power	Petroleum	Natural gas	Solar Wind Hydropower Nuclear Biomass

Figure 12.1 Classification of energy resources and technologies according to their carbon intensities

know. History seems to suggest that Chinese policymakers will eventually do the right thing, but in many cases only after they try a lot of wrong ideas first.

Former U.S. President Barack Obama argued that the market forces drive the decoupling of emissions and economic growth in the United States, and that the global momentum of clean energy is irreversible (Obama, 2017). He may be right about America, but what happens in America does not necessarily constitute global momentum. In the arena of energy and CO_2 emissions, China is now by far a bigger player than the United States. The low-carbon transition in China is predominantly guided by the state, and the momentum may be quite reversible. There are tremendous embedded interests in high-carbon and ultra-high-carbon industries in China. The momentum of clean energy development in China could stop if Chinese leaders relax their attention on low-carbon transition. Because China emits twice as much CO_2 as the United States, a high-carbon scenario in China will more than cancel out whatever reduction the United States could possibly achieve. Whatever President Obama's legacy may be, it will be dwarfed by the impacts of China.

The Western media have praised China for its leadership in developing renewable energy and improving efficiency at amazing speed. They also have blamed China for its insatiable demand for dirty fossil fuels and huge greenhouse gas emissions. In some ways, China looks like an angel, and in other ways, a demon. I am hoping this book will deliver a relatively fair and accurate image of the Chinese people. They are neither angels nor demons. They are just humans.

Reference

Obama, B., 2017. The irreversible momentum of clean energy. *Science* 355, 126–129.

Appendix
Useful data sources

BP Statistical Review of World Energy: www.bp.com/en/global/corporate/
energy-economics/statistical-review-of-world-energy.html

China Coal Industry Association: www.coalchina.org.cn/ (in Chinese only)

China Electricity Council: http://english.cec.org.cn/

China Photovoltaic Industry Association: www.chinapv.org.cn/ (in Chinese
only)

China Urban-Rural Construction Statistical Yearbooks: www.mohurd.gov.
cn/xytj/tjzljsxytjgb/jstjnj/index.html (Web pages only in Chinese, statistical tables contain both Chinese and English titles)

China Wind Energy Association: www.cwea.org.cn/ (in Chinese only)

National Bureau of Statistics of China: http://data.stats.gov.cn/english/

World Bank: http://databank.worldbank.org/

Index

For Product Safety Concerns and Information please contact our
EU representative GPSR@taylorandfrancis.com Taylor & Francis
Verlag GmbH, Kaufingerstraße 24, 80331 München, Germany